JOYCE DRURY

"WE WERE THERE"

The Jupiter Press

First published in Great Britain in 1997 by

The Jupiter Press

Oracle House

1 - 3 Gospel End Road

Sedgley, Dudley

West Midlands

DY3 3LT

Printed by

Holloway Design & Print

Holloway House,

Martin Hill Street,

Dudley,

West Midlands

DY2 8RT

ISBN 0 9530620 0 7

CONTENTS

Drawings by Marcelle Dawson nee Grennan

FOREWORD

As Centre Organiser for Torquay of the British Red Cross, I welcome the privilege and opportunity to write a few words of introduction to this book, on the role of the VAD during the War.

I have long felt that insufficient recognition had been given to the part that the VAD (Voluntary Aid Detachments) played during the 1939-1945 War.

As we pass the 50th Anniversary of VE and VJ days, it is most appropriate that such a book should be published, for it coincides with the 125th Anniversary of the British Red Cross.

In commending this book, I much hope that it will be widely read, not only by members of the Red Cross, but by the general public, and that it will make a significant contribution to the 50th Anniversary Celebrations, alongside those of the 125th Anniversary of the British Red Cross.

Kenneth R S Wickins
31st October 1995

British Red Cross
Torquay Centre
77 Abbey Road
TORQUAY
S Devon

INTRODUCTION

'This delightful book of Mrs Drury's which includes anecdotes and illustrations from other ex-VADs makes fascinating reading for anyone, but particularly for those of us who had the privilege of serving with the Royal Navy at such a vital time in history. It is going to travel all over this country and all over the world and perhaps it will stir up memories among some who used to be VADs and went through similar experiences all those years ago.

For this reason it may be of interest to know that there is in existence a VAD (RN) Association which is extremely successful in organising reunions where sometimes people meet again and recognise each other after nearly half a century. We have annual gatherings in London and in different parts of the British Isles and these are unusually friendly, sympathetic occasions, perhaps because of the challenges we all had to face as VADs when we were young. There is also a Newsletter circulated twice a year and on Remembrance Sunday a contingent joins in the parade at the Cenotaph where one of our members offers a wreath.

Mrs Sheila Eastell of Church Cottage, Itchingfield, Horsham, West Sussex is our honorary secretary and anyone joining can be assured of a warm welcome into what I believe to be a very special association.'

Lady Arbuthnot
Founder President
VAD (RN) ASSOCIATION

February 15th, 1995

BRIEF HISTORY OF THE VADs

In 1908 the Territorial Army was formed to support the regular Army. In addition, the following year, the VAD came into being, to provide additional Nurses in the event of war.

The VAD, originally BRCS, was later joined by St John and St Andrew.

A small number of VADs obtained their first experience of war in the Balkans in 1912.

At the outbreak of the First World War in 1914, about 14,000 women in 180 detachments were serving. Amongst their duties were the escort of seriously injured, manning dressing stations, assisting doctors, cooking, and helping to man 1,400 Emergency Hospitals.

Katherine Furse led a pioneer band of ladies to France in 1914 - she had already formed the VAD in readiness before the War.

In 1917 when the Admiralty wanted to form the WRNS it was to Katherine Furse (later Dame Katherine Furse) they turned - she became the first Director WRNS, bringing other VADs with her to form the HQ Staff.

Many VADs served overseas in Europe, the Mediterranean and North Africa - there were also units from the Dominions.

Some VADs contracted with the War Office to serve for £20 per annum - with free board and lodging and 1st Class travel - and to rank immediately after the QAIMNS. In all, 126,000 served during the War, of whom 245 were killed.

After the War the service reorganised to supplement the Medical Services of HM Hospitals - the VAD would remain Mobile - the immobile formed the Nursing Auxiliaries of the Second World War.

In the Second World War 15,000 members enlisted in Britain in the Army, Navy and RAF, and 2,000 were released to local Nursing Reserves.

In 1944 the Army VAD were absorbed into ATS/QAs Nursing Orderlies. A few joined another service.

The RAF eventually disbanded their VADs.

The Royal Navy kept their VADs, plus some from the Army and the RAF, until 1960, when they were absorbed by the QARNNS.

The VAD (RN) performed many tasks - they manned Hospital Ships, provided Cooks, Lab Assistants, Nurses, Medical Secretaries, X-Ray and Operating Theatre staff. In fact they filled in the many and varied duties that needed to be done.

Between 1917 and 1960 approximately 5,800 VADs served with the Royal Navy.

Kindly supplied by (VAD) RN Association

DEDICATION

This book is dedicated to the teenagers and young women who put their careers on hold to staff the service hospitals as nurses.

They left their secure homes and everything they had known for an unknown way of life to give much needed nursing and care to thousands of young servicemen.

Joyce Drury

Joyce (Billie) Drury nee Saunders

Everyone knows boys were called up for National Service at eighteen during the war, but it is not generally known that girls were called up at nineteen. Unless you were a mother or in a reserved occupation, you were directed into the services or work of national importance.

From sixteen it was fire-watching for your road or street. You were required to learn how to put incendiary bombs out and had to work a rota for aid raid warnings day and night. I think at eighteen you could become an air raid warden. I had already decided to go into one of the services as a VAD (Voluntary Aid Detachment) at nineteen and Miss Earle, my Commandant, put my name forward for the Royal Navy.

Joyce (Billie) Drury nee Saunders
VAD (RN) 1942-45

All females had to go for an interview at the Ministry of Labour two months before their nineteenth birthday. These women interviewers regarded themselves as a 'General' who had complete power. At my interview I expect, being a teenager, I was a bit cocky and told my lady interviewer that she didn't really need to see me as I was already going in the services as a VAD. "Oh no," said she, "I am directing you into the Civil Nursing Reserve". (I found out later that it was a 'feather in her cap' if she could get anyone for the CNR especially out of ladies hairdressing). "Further interview next week!".

As soon as I got out of the office, I telephoned Miss Earle, "Silly woman, don't worry, she can't do this", she said. The following week I went back for the second interview after fuming for seven days. "Oh yes, I've had a phone call about you. You're going into the Royal Navy. I don't need to see you anymore." I often wonder what Miss Earle said to her. She was definitely subdued. I don't know how these women got away with being so bumptious. There was a war on, women were needed and it was their job to get them. I know they annoyed a lot of people.

I joined the Red Cross when I was seventeen and became a member of the 'Devon 6th' detachment. I took my tests in first aid, home nursing etc. I volunteered to go mobile in November 1942 and had my experience hours at

My mother and I when I was on my way to join the Royal Navy. Poor mother, she used to worry about me being in Plymouth. They could see in Torquay when we were having air raids because the sky would be lit up all over that area. There would be a note on the letter board after a raid, *'Your father telephoned to see if you were safe.'* **I expect he worried just as much as mother but would never have admitted it.**

the Torbay Hospital. At that time, nineteen years was the minimum age for going mobile, which meant going into the services. I was accepted as a RNVAD (Royal Navy Voluntary Aid Detachment) on my nineteenth birthday and bought the rest of my uniform - the VADs had to buy their own uniform which were supplied in those days by Rockeys in Fleet Street, Torquay. After our initial layout for uniform, the RN allowed us ten pounds a year for upkeep. I passed my local medical and had to report on 3rd January 1943 to the Royal Navy Hospital, Plymouth. My mother was quite upset when, two days before I was to report, a wing of the hospital at the RNH was bombed. There were many ambulances evacuating patients to Newton Abbott where there was a service hospital. 'Mothers always tend to worry', I thought then, but I probably would have been just the same if it had been my children!

It was a whole new life. I was now in the Royal Navy. Everyone was very kind. I met my Commandant, who was in charge at the VAD Quarters situated in Mannamead, Plymouth. Several big houses had been taken over for Quarters. We slept two, three or four to a room depending on its size. Transport was laid on by the Royal Navy to take nurses to the hospital and back as necessary.

My first morning on duty was 'electric'. The wards had forty beds. The medical officer was on his morning round. When doing so, he had all the ward staff around him and orders were given concerning treatment. The sirens blew for an air raid but the MO continued with his round. The ward was silent. This was how it was with the Royal Navy. When the MO was present for his rounds, the ratings were at attention in bed. Big guns opened up - woom - woom - woom. Fire parties laid their hoses down the ward. Still the round went on. No-one made a murmur or showed any fright. As the round finished half an hour later, the all clear was sounded. This happened many times at later dates but this was my first morning!

All the wards had bricked up windows for the air raids. If a raid became heavy, all up-patients were moved to shelters. Our orders were that if there were any patients that couldn't be moved, we were to put a mattress over them and get underneath the bed ourselves. As long as you were with a very sick patient, even when the raids were very noisy, they would not panic. Thinking back, it was easy to understand this. All the VADs looked calm and attractive in their uniforms and the men did not want to show fear in front of them.

When I first arrived in the Royal Navy, there were many Sick Berth Attendants (SBAs) on the wards. Each ward had a senior SBA over it for RN administration, with a Sister over the nursing staff. As the weeks went on, most of the SBAs went to sea and more VADs were coming in to take their place.

After three months, I was passed as Grade I. A month later, I was drafted to Maristow RNH near Roborough just outside Plymouth. It still belonged to the RNH; Plymouth was like an annexe. Maristow was very remote. The drive was three miles long, then you were on the moor! This was a mansion house and the rooms were wards; ground floor surgical, first floor medical. The staff were all very pleasant, like one big family, which was just as well as there was nothing to do socially. There was tennis and most of us liked walking - it was beautiful countryside. There was one transport out each day, which left RNH Plymouth at 9.30 pm to bring us back. Sometimes the off-duty nurses would go to a dance in Plymouth and get a taxi back. Even then we had to 'chat up' the taxi driver so he would take us down the drive, which was dark with a sheer drop on one side and down hill and they did not like going down there.

Taken at Marstow on the tennis courts. *(Left to Right - Myself, Charlie and Joan Candy).* **Charlie was a footman at Buckingham Palace before he was an SBA. I don't think they were married until after this photograph was taken. Some time after the war, I saw a magazine with Windsor Castle featured and Charlie Candy was photographed as controller in charge of the footmen. It was nice to know he had survived the war and I hope Joan did too. They were a lovely couple and both good nurses.**

We had a Superintending Sister who was in charge of the female nursing staff. She was also in charge of our catering. We were normally well fed, but here we were not. She hoarded food, which she was not allowed to do, then when ENSA came to entertain the patients she would give a lavish party or entertain the nursing staff from the American base a few miles away. They were all entertained on the female staff's rations! There were four of us she always invited to these parties because we had good personalities and could mix with her guests. We certainly used to eat well at these dinner parties. Even the MO told her we were not being fed properly. There were only about fourteen VADs there

Bridget and I with leading SBA Mann with whom we got along very well. Bridget and I were good friends while we were together.

at this time but at the end of the year, there were many more as the SBAs were sent to the ships and abroad. I heard later that she had been reported to our Commandant in Plymouth and the catering was taken out of her hands. This was after I had gone back to RNH Plymouth.

In the May, my sister was getting married in Torquay. I was on night duty which meant twenty eight nights, twelve hours on, twelve hours off, with no break. We all just did this with no argument! I needed to come off on the Friday morning. My friend, who was following on nights, would do the Friday night for me. 'No!'. This same dear Supt. Sister would not let me although my ward Sister agreed I could go. I think this lady was very bitter about life in general. My ward Sister told me to go off at 7 am instead of 8 am. There was an old Chief Petty Officer with a car and he took me up the drive to the main road. Then I hitch-hiked. I was on the moor. A lot of men were working at the dockyard and came in everyday. I got in a car with three men , (imagine doing that these days) and when I told them where I was going, they dropped me at the bus stop for Torquay. I caught the 8.25 am bus which would get there by 10.10 am. The wedding was at 10.30 am! So, here I was on my way to be a bridesmaid. I had managed to get washed in the early hours, so I only needed to get changed. Luckily, the bus got in on time. A car was waiting for me at the bus station. Off with my uniform, let my hair down, put on my bridesmaid's dress, all in a quarter of an hour! After the wedding and the reception, I had two hours sleep before we all went to the Spa ballroom to a tea dance. Then dancing again at night. I slept late on Sunday, then back to Plymouth on Sunday evening.

Left to Right - Back Row - Elspeth Robertson, Joan Candy, Nurse Fawcett, Bridget. Front Sister Smith, **who was a good sister, very strict but would laugh with us. I liked her. Then** *Superintending Sister Jones-Davies,* **who was in charge of the nursing staff and our catering!!! at Maristow.**

There were quite a few eventful things to happen before I left Maristow. We were kept very busy but it was a happy place, even allowing for our Supt. Sister. At the beginning of June, one patient asked me if I could do anything to help him. He was getting married in a week's time and here he was in hospital with a bullet wound across his shoulder. He had asked the MO and he had refused permission. Everything was ready for the wedding as he should have been on leave, but his ship had been hit on the way home to port. It was not easy getting food together for a wedding in 1943, so he really should be there. I got on very well with the Sister and the MO so I asked them if we could talk about this. The MO was afraid he would go sick on shore. I said that the patient had promised me not to do this. "Well nurse, if you think he won't and you can strap him up to last five days, I'll let him go, but if he does not come back on time, you will be in trouble." (My dressings never slipped. I often remembered the old ex-army doctor who gave me my Red Cross first aid exam. He told me my bandage would keep my dressing on but would not win a competition!). I had a talk with this young man, telling him what the MO had said. He swore he would come back. I strapped his shoulder to last five days, told him not to let anyone pat him on the back, wished him good luck and hoped! He returned after five days with a piece of wedding cake and a lovely letter to me from his bride thanking me for speaking for him.

At the beginning of August, the Daily Mirror held a garden party for the patients. All the surgical ward patients were brought out in their beds with canopies over for the sun. The up-patients were out, either walking or in wheel chairs. I was working on the bed patients when the photographer asked the Sister for three nurses for a photo. "You, you and you". So this was how I came to be on the centre page of the Daily Mirror on 8th August 1943. The photographer had six fit up-patients and they had to chair carry us in a race. The caption read, *"Hospital patients' dream - to pick up one's nurse and run off with her. These*

Hospital patient's dream —to pick up one's nurse and run off with her. These nurses are thoroughly enjoying being run off with—and even Sister smiles in approval. For the men are Navy casualties who have coaxed nurse into a bandy-chair race down the lawn just to show how well .hey are. It's sports day at the new naval hospital at Lord Roborough's house at Maristow, South Devon, and every man who can hobble or can be wheeled out in his plaster cast or bed cage is on the terrace to watch.

This was the Daily Mirror garden party. (Left to right - of the three VAD nurses Funnel, Saunders and Macdonald). In the background is Sister Davies. On the left the patients were mostly from H.M.S. Melbreek. This was a newspaper photograph.

nurses are thoroughly enjoying being run off with ... even Sister smiles in approval. For the men are Navy casualties who have coaxed nurse into a bandy-chair race down the lawn just to show how well they are. It's sports day at the new Naval hospital at Lord Roborough's house at Maristow, South Devon and every man who can hobble or can be wheeled out in his plaster cast or bed cage is on the terrace to watch." I had letters from friends on ships as far away as Malta, Gibraltar and Iceland, who had seen this photograph. The Daily Mirror got around!

This is a snapshot taken at the same party.

It was different to working in hospitals today. All syringes, needles and instruments had to be sterilised in the sterilisers on the ward; dressings had to be cut and prepared on the ward, put in big drums and sent to be sterilised. This had to be done in our spare time! It must have been successful - we didn't get cross infections and wounds healed well. We always wore masks when doing dressings and scrubbed up for each one. Everything was in short supply and we never wasted anything. Bits of cotton wool were always used up in the drums for swabs; bits of bandage for small dressings.

In September 1943, one of our nurses went down with diphtheria. There was quite a panic on as we were nursing a lot of post-diphtheria patients from a ship that had been hit with it. When the fever was at its height in RNH a bomb had hit their ward and they were thrown out of bed. It had affected them all very badly. They had to lie flat in bed for three months. So it was thought there must be a carrier amongst them. Everyone had swabs taken. They were clear and all nurses were clear. As an after-thought our Wren steward who waited at table was swabbed! She was the carrier, so we had to consider ourselves lucky we didn't all catch it. Our nurse did recover.

We used to have alternate weekends off, one from Friday afternoon to Sunday night, the other from Saturday midday to Sunday night. On this short weekend, most times I would take one of the other girls with me to Torquay for some of them who lived in places like Carlisle it was not very nice being stuck at Maristow instead of being able to go home. My parents always made them welcome and Torquay was a nice place for a break. One of the times when I went back on my own, I could not get a taxi. They were not very plentiful and with the Americans around they preferred to take them! (I wonder why!). I had to get back from the station to the RNH to pick up my transport to Maristow. It was blackout and I had to walk along Union Street alone. I knew there would be plenty of shore patrols (RN police) so if I had any trouble I could call for help. Several sailors came up to me but I ignored them until I had one each side! When they discovered I was a nurse going to the hospital, they said I could not walk down there on my own so they would escort me. When we got to the

Ida Wray *(left),* **who came from Carlisle, came home with me a few times and was a friend over some months. The other VAD came as well that weekend but I can't recall her name.**

hospital, I thanked them and said good-bye. They found there was a pub next to the RNH and off they went for a drink.

We had all nationalities to nurse so it could be difficult when they could not speak any English. On one occasion at Maristow, we had two Poles, a Dane, two Frenchmen, a Czech and a Belgian in one of the rooms. The Belgian could speak French and Dutch and they all seemed to get into conversation together with the young Belgian translating for them. It was quite amusing sometimes although we nurses knew they were having conversations about us!

These patients had been in for months and were now going on leave. We were both sorry and pleased to see them go. The tall young man at the back with no hat is Norwegian. As he spoke only a little English we knew practically nothing about his background, he was really very sweet and everyone liked him. Nurses Candy, Saunders, Hawken, Macdonald and our Sister's in the front whose name eludes me.

The same patients in hospital uniform with nurse Grove-Jones *at the back, Middle row* **Saunders and Andrews,** *on the front* **nurse Hawken.**

The thing I found very sad was nursing servicemen with cancer. Somehow you expected them to get wounded and there were many medical cases from immersion in the sea when ships had been sunk, but cancer I found difficult to accept. One young boy of seventeen, whom we nursed who died, stood out in my mind, also a big Marine I had to special watch (like intensive care) in RNH Plymouth who had been so strong and fearless to have to die like that.

In November, I returned to RNH Plymouth. I had made some good friends at Maristow whom I was sorry to leave, but really I was quite glad to leave Maristow before Winter really came. Things went on very much the same. I was on duty for Christmas and they really tried to give the patients a good time, begging and borrowing all over! Then the ones who had been on duty for Christmas were off for the New Year. We had nurses coming in now in bigger numbers, I think into 1944 they began to accept the VADs at seventeen and a half so there were more available.

We came off night duty at 8 am but didn't always take the transport back to Mannamead for breakfast. We did twenty eight nights duty with no break at this time. I think they got a break in this at a later date but doing twelve hours on and off didn't really give us much leisure. I used to pay a visit to the Officer's Club on the Hoe where we had a leisurely breakfast which was very pleasant, then a walk on the Plymouth Hoe, the Sound below with the ships, the Sunderland flying boats skimming the water as they took off. It made me wonder sometimes what the Sound had looked like when Sir Francis Drake played bowls waiting for the Spanish Armada.

The night duty meals we were given left a lot to be desired. When I could I went to visit my friend Rene from Torquay who worked in a butcher's on the outskirts of Plymouth (her husband worked in the dockyard during the war). Then I came back with a supper which was quite a 'banquet' for my night colleague and myself, there was always sufficient for the Night Sister as well. This was quite a treat in those days of rationing and, of course, quite illegal.

I think it was 1944 when the War Office allowed the church bells to ring again. Previously they were kept for the warning of invasion and rung only as an alarm. This was very bad for the night staff as there was a church nearby in Mannamead. What with bell ringers practice, weddings, funerals and all the weekend services, the days were very disturbed for night staff. There was really no way of avoiding bells even with cotton wool in our ears!

On one occasion when I was on night duty, I had a seventeen year old patient who was very ill with a bone infection and in a lot of pain. All my spare time at night I sat by his bed and held his hand. "This is what my mother would do, nurse," the boy said. He made a good recovery and was transferred to a convalescent hospital. The day he went the Roman Catholic Padre came to me and said, "I know what you have done for that boy nurse, I won't forget it". After which he treated me with great respect although I was Church of England, and went out of his way to help me whenever he could. Some months later I was walking through Devonport Barracks when a tall, young sailor came up to me. "Remember me nurse?", he said. It was the same boy who had been so ill, he was off back to sea and was about to join his ship. I hope he survived after recovering from such an illness.

Another young man comes to mind who had a gas-gangrene of the wall of his stomach. I was on night duty with him as a patient. This was a case that was not expected to survive. Normally they would amputate in such a condition but this was not a limb. Continually changing the dressings and careful nursing plus a miracle from above saved his life. This was before we had penicillin and as his wife was expecting twins at the time I was so please for her that he recovered.

There were many more cases similar to these in the time I spent as a VAD but these really stood out in my mind.

In February of 1944, the Matron sent for me. I wondered what I had done wrong for Matron to send for me. As I waited outside her office, thoughts were flying through my head. "Sit down nurse", she said - it couldn't be trouble or I would be standing. "I have decided to make you a senior VAD, you will be the youngest in the Plymouth Command. The reports we have had from the doctors and Sisters show you are capable." I was completely taken by surprise. There had been no hint of this from any source. I was very pleased because although I would have more responsibility, I would have more privileges. I would no longer have to be in by ten thirty or ask for a late pass. There were other things as well which made life more pleasant. It did not please some, who were a lot older, to think I had been given promotion over them. I felt a bit sorry but I could do nothing about this.

In the early summer of 1944, I was told the Matron wanted me on the telephone. I thought they were joking, Matron didn't ask to speak to VADs on the telephone, it was always you who went to her office. It was like God asking to speak to the vicar! Well, it was Matron, "I'm sorry to do this to you nurse, I am sending you thirty new VADs on to your ward. I know you are busy but I want you to show these young ladies the ropes and lick them into shape." I was amazed that she should speak to me and I suppose flattered that she thought I could do this. We had lost all our working SBAs from the ward and were very short of nurses. It was a very busy ward. Between us we showed them what we were doing, set some to filling our dressing drums and generally got some routine into chaos. After a couple of days, I told them to get their hair off their collars and to cut out the lipstick, for lipstick on a mask was not something that was allowed. "Who does she think she is?", said one of the new intakes, thinking I was just the same level as them. The nurse she asked said, "Well, you see that red flash on her arm, that tells you why she can tell you what to do." This shows how things had changed. When I arrived, there was only me that week and we were coming in in ones, now we were so short of nurses they were coming in in thirties. They spent about two weeks with me. I might add that I met some of these young ladies at various times and they were all very good nurses. Quite a few laughed at their first days with me.

One day, about 6.30 pm, a visitor came to see one of the seriously ill patients. It was the young sailor's father. After seeing the patient the father came to me and told me off. Apparently he had received a letter that day putting his son on the SCL ('serious case list' - not about to die but very ill). He said that his wife had been very upset about this letter and he could not see that he was any worse than yesterday. He lived in Plymouth and had seen him the day before. I told him he had better come and see the Sister in the morning. When I went to see the patient after the father's visit, the boy asked me if he was going to die. He was about nineteen. His father had shown him the letter from the Admiralty! I had to think very fast and told him that after so many days in hospital all parents were informed. I said that it was a routine letter and the fact that he lived in Plymouth and his parents knew he was in hospital had been overlooked. This satisfied him and he settled down again. That father got into so much trouble the next day with the Sister for telling his son about the letter and upsetting him, also for being rude to her nurse and she said that if he 'was in any further trouble he would have no more visiting rights'. She was a very nice Sister, real Royal Navy, but she was so cross with this man when I told her what he had done.

Most of the Sisters were good to work under. We helped each other in a lot of ways and they depended on us. Occasionally we would get a newly passed SRN who had come into the RN with her new rank, who had no idea how much work we did and soon found out how much they had to depend on us, both on the wards and to learn the Royal Navy routine. It was different from a civilian hospital. They were as short of Sisters as nurses and they wanted them on the wards fast, letting them train in the routine under a Senior Sister with the help of the nurses. I suppose, coming from a civilian hospital, they would regard us as untrained helps. I don't know what they thought VADs did, or who would do the nursing if we didn't. The RN Sisters soon explained and it was not long before they were treating us with respect. All VADs ranked as officers in the RN lived as officers and travelled on first class warrants.

The Royal Navy was the first to get penicillin. It had wonderful results. We had used sulphothizal and sulphonamide. Now it was mostly replaced. When we first started to use it, we could not understand why our hands were smelling of bad body odour. We discovered it was from the syringe when giving a penicillin injection! The penicillin cleared up infections of all types in a shorter period thus patients recovered at a faster rate. Another problem it solved was venereal disease. It had been taking as long as two years on injections to clear it up often getting jaundice on the way from the drug as a side effect. Now it was cleared up in six weeks. You may think that it would be their own fault for getting VD. Yes, it was, but young men of seventeen and eighteen were away from home for the first time, putting into ports, having too much to drink and falling prey to prostitutes. Their case cards showed it was usually a prostitute who infected them. Two years of treatment was a long punishment. Experienced men very rarely got infected and they were put on a charge if they did.

Now I was on draft again. I was sharing a room with five Senior VADs and we were working on the wards but knew we would be moving. One evening they came back to our room and said, "Our names are on the board to report, we

These were taken in the ward of the sick bay at HMS Impregnable with some of the SBAs that took care of me while I was there.They look serious but I can tell you we had a lot of laughs.

are all going to Nairobi, expect you will be coming with us". When I reported to the Commandant, she told me I was going to HMS Impregnable. When I asked where this was, she replied that it was St Budeaux which was on the outskirts of Plymouth above Devonport dockyard. I was the only one going there. It was a lone draft. The sick bay on the camp had thirteen men and I was the only woman working with them. The reason there was one female nurse was because there were a few Wrens working on the camp and if there were any accidents I attended and I also saw to their sick parades. If they were sick they went to hospital. It was quite interesting. We did inoculations, various treatments for the seamen and there was a short term sickbay. We had two Medical Officers and thirteen sick berth attendants of different ranks plus me. One period, the whole sick bay had to work blood grouping a thousand men before they went to sea. I got on very well with the men and I can't say I had any problems being the only female among so many of them. I made friends with a couple of Wren Petty Officers. We used to go out together and they often came to Torquay for a weekend. There was always plenty to do in St Budeaux. There were always plenty of dances and some nice little pubs in the area. In fact, all the time I was in the RN I worked hard but I played hard too.

Right - **Marjorie Muxworthy later Rhys.**
Centre - **she was Chief Petty Officer on the camp and a very special friend.**

On one occasion I had to give evidence at a Court Marshall. It was like being in a film. The Commodore sat in the middle of a table flanked by officers. I'd never seen so much 'spit and polish' or so much gold braid! Those giving evidence had to go into the room one at a time and stand in front of their table. I wasn't frightened but I was very impressed. Whenever I see this scene in a film I say to myself, 'You did this for real!'.

I only experienced sexual harassment once during the time I was in the Royal Navy . The Medical Officer was on leave and another came as a replacement for two weeks. He had a red beard and was rather a wolf. His first words to me were, "You'll look after me while I'm here won't you?", with a glint in his eye! Talk about being pursued! The Chief Petty Officer told the Senior Medical Officer, because the men I worked with regarded me as a younger member of their own family. The SMO asked me if I wanted to make a complaint but I told him that I could manage for two weeks. This man thought he was irresistible to females. I don't think he had worked with VADs in a sick bay before. We all had a good laugh after he had gone. I had to deal with a few tricky situations, but I was never left alone with him. All sailors flirt with the females but this was much more. He would have been in a lot of trouble had I put a complaint forward to the SMO. The Matron of RNH, who I was still under, would have had him on a charge. I could not refuse to work with him, but I could refuse a 'date', which I did. I never came across a situation like this again nor did I meet this doctor at any other place.

One day, one of the seamen brought a cat into the sick bay. It was going mad with its mouth. We wrapped it in a towel to protect us from its claws, two held it while we opened its mouth and found a fish bone jammed across the roof of its mouth. So we became vets for a few minutes and removed the bone with forceps, swabbed its mouth with saline, then sent it on its way. The cat was very pleased and seemed to say thank you! It was nice to think in the middle of a war that people still cared enough to help an animal in trouble.

We were inoculating all the seamen up to date getting them ready for joining the ships for 'D' Day. The 'buzz' was there all the time. Plymouth and the surrounding area was packed with all nationalities. Small craft lay all the way up the creek under HMS Impregnable. Everywhere we went was packed. All the pubs were short of drinks. Some would open for only one or two hours a day. You couldn't have what you asked for - you had what they could offer. Sometimes they would let the customers have one drink each and that was it. This applied to soft drinks as well. The dance halls were packed. There weren't a lot because Plymouth was more or less flattened.

We were still getting air raid warnings. It was not so much bombing raids as observation planes trying to find out what was going on. The Germans knew we would invade but they didn't know when. If the warning sounded at night, we had to run fast to our raid station because the smoke screens would be belching smoke. We would get lost in the black smoke and dirty! I kept seaman's trousers and jersey to get dressed at speed because getting caught in the smoke was horrible. The smoke screens were at the top of the camp which was high on the hill. The smoke covered the camp and the creek.

This was a peculiar time. Everything was waiting. We all knew what for but we didn't really talk about it. We had been taught well. 'Careless talk costs lives'. My sister's brother-in-law was sent to the United States Navy for a short trip, probably because he could speak French and Flemish. Ambrose Egan visited me at HMS Impregnable as the US ship was laid in the river underneath us. It was nice to see him and he brought me fruit off his ship that I hadn't seen for years. The US services went short of nothing. They brought all their supplies with them. We had quite a few nights out together and enjoyed ourselves with lots of fun and laughs. We lived in this strange vacuum for a few weeks until that night on the run up to 'D' Day.

It was June 5th, 1944. We knew that 'D' Day was nigh. Everyone was confined to camp. There was no shore leave. The small craft had been anchored in 'threes' all the way up the creek for weeks, waiting. On the night of June 6th, this had changed. They were now side by side in single file ready to peel off for sea. As I looked down on this historic phenomenon I wondered how many of these small craft would survive. Next morning, the 7th, the creek was empty. It was an eerie feeling. We knew it had begun.

This shore station was being used for re-ammunitioning the ships. We had nothing to do but wait. There was a film being shown in the drill hall, 'The Rains Came' (I'll always remember that film). The idea was to keep the ratings together for their calls. Most ratings and the sick bay staff attended. As we watched, the bugle sounded in the drill hall for the first ammunitioning party to report, (they used the tally ho call), then the next and the next and so on until there was only sick bay staff left in the hall. It ran successfully for these parties. We had very few casualties to deal with from the ammunition parties. I shall never forget this. It was a memorable day. One we had been waiting for. The whole country took part whether fighting force or civilian. Some were in more danger but none could function without the others. Was it really fifty years ago?

After 'D' Day, we were still kept busy. Life went on much the same. We had a young Petty Officer in the sick bay for a fortnight with an infection. He asked me to his wedding. He was marrying a Plymouth girl. He came from the North of Scotland. His parents were coming down but there was no one else on his side, only one or two of his RN friends. It was not easy to travel or get away during the war. I said that I would go to the church but didn't think I would go to the reception as I didn't know anyone except the bridegroom. He was to marry the daughter of a publican of a big hotel. When I got to the church I was met by two Petty Officers who had been told to look after me and take me to the reception. It was a very big affair. I must say it was a good job I had a strong stomach. Every time I drank half a glass it was filled again. This was in a time of great shortage! They must have been saving the bottles for quite a time! After the reception I prepared to go back to camp. "Oh no", they all said. A taxi had been ordered for me from their hotel. It was a little difficult to say no with such hospitality. The hotel was closed for the night. Another meal was laid on and at least I could control what I was drinking as we collected it ourselves from the bar. At about 11 pm the taxi came to take me and a couple of POs back to the camp. The driver said he was in no hurry, he was enjoying the party. There were no drink drive rules in those days but I didn't want a drunk driver driving me six miles back to camp, so after ten minutes I said, "Let's go". He was a bit disappointed! We got back safely and quite 'merry'. Everyone had had a good time. It was quite a wedding, even by peace time standards but this was 1944 with the war and rationing still on! This was the biggest wedding I had been to during the war. I was pleased I went to support the bridegroom's family. I was made so welcome and it was quite a party!

Normal dining out in Plymouth was not an easy affair and the menu would not suit diners today. It was usual to queue to get into a cafe or restaurant. In 1945 the NAAFI opened a large services club in Plymouth but until then it was most difficult. Some restaurants were better than others but all frugal. I've eaten whale steaks (I wouldn't now). A lot of the menus were vegetarian as meat was in very short supply, mostly one course and tea or coffee. I often got invited to cocktail parties on board the ships, from battleships to motor torpedo boats, which were like motor launches. I mixed with people and had friends from all walks of life. Although I worked hard I did have a good time too!

We were moving now into 1945. The Royal Navy was sending a lot of ships and men to the East so the camp had a lot of men coming through for inoculations

My wedding was arranged in just one week. I telephoned my father on Thursday, got leave on Monday and my family had everything arranged. The Church at Upton, the special licence, the reception, the wedding cake, everything was ready. This was quite something in 1945 as everything was very difficult and in short supply. Even photographs were difficult *(I know a lot of people who got married in the war who do not have photographs of their wedding which was rather sad).* **I was lucky. One friend, an amateur photographer, Arthur Warman, took a lot of photographs for me and a friend at Bathes, the photographic people, enlarged them. Also Mr Cousteau** *(father of Jacques Cousteau, the television underwater photographer)* **took a whole set of photos and gave them to us. These were developed on French Ministry of Propaganda paper!! There weren't any coupons for a wedding dress. Service weddings were fashionable and we all looked very nice. Best man was my sister's husband, Lt. Patrick Egan, my sister Mary was matron of honour, Petty Officer Miriam Russell (Russ) and Doris, who later married Cam, Patrick's brother, were bridesmaids. Then my dear Leslie who died in 1979. It was a lovely wedding. This photo was taken by Mr Cousteau.**

etc., ready for joining ship. I was kept busy. I also met my future husband, Leslie, about this time and I didn't know him very long before I married him. I got married on June 7th 1945, and we were happily married until his death in 1979. Shortly after the wedding I was drafted to RNH Plymouth. So it was back to the wards. I had enjoyed my stay at HMS Impregnable and had made a lot of friends. That was Royal Navy life. You made good friends and then had to move on. Some you kept in touch with, others just faded out of your life, which seems a bit sad really.

This is my father and I going into the church. The taxi driver 'Clem' arranged the taxis, these again were difficult to come by. He also booked our honeymoon for us at a country hotel at Maidencombe and wouldn't tell any of the others where he was taking us. Many of our friends tried all sorts of bribery at the party after we had gone. This photograph was taken by Arthur Warman.

I was back to ward duties. About September time I applied for my discharge from the Royal Navy. Being married I was entitled to 'Demob'. I was called to the office and a Superintending Sister interviewed me. "You can't have your discharge nurse", she said, "so will you sign this form". I looked at the form and it was a re-signing for another year. I told her 'no'. "Your husband has gone to Australia", she said, "there is a draft of nurses going there, you can go on it if you wish." (Leslie had asked me not to apply for this. I think he wanted to think I was safe at home! He knew he wouldn't be staying in Australia and as it happened he went to Hong Kong as the Japanese moved out). This Superintending Sister had me standing in front of her for one hour trying to persuade me. I suppose I was a good nurse and she had orders not to let me go. The war with Germany was over and the one with the Japanese was ending. I had decided it was time to became a civilian. Supt. Sister asked me to stay and do a month's night duty and I agreed to do so. Apparently I could have gone that day but she had been told not to let me go. I hope she didn't get into much trouble for not succeeding. I think if she had approached it differently and said to me, 'You're a good nurse, we want to keep you a bit longer', she might have succeeded, but trying to trick me into signing annoyed me.

So, by the end of 1945, I was back in Torquay and out of the Royal Navy. I missed the Navy life and the friendships which went with it and it took a while to settle back to civilian life.

I hope you have found my three years as a Red Cross RNVAD an enlightening bit of history. I can only say I enjoyed it and if I had not married I would have been there perhaps a little longer. It was certainly an experience I would not have missed and I am very proud to have been a British Red Cross RNVAD.

Drawn by Alice Brereton-Smith nee Ruttledge.

Sheila Eastell nee Hamlyn

This is the first of memoirs from my VAD colleagues. I start with Sheila because she comes from Torquay. As far as we know we did not meet although we were part of Torquay BRC Society. She was in Devon 26th Detachment, I was in Devon 6th. There was also Devon 22nd and there was friendly rivalry between us all. Each thought their Detachment was the best and of course they were to us!

She is at present secretary to the VAD (RN) Association which is over 500 strong. There are regular meetings taking place not just in the British Isles but in other parts of the world.

Joyce Drury

My Service with the VAD (RN)

Sheila Eastell
"1947 after Trinco"

I was born and brought up at St Marychurch, Torquay and attended first the St Marychurch C of E School and then the Torquay Grammar. When I was 16, I joined the No.26 Detachment of the British Red Cross Society and did my Home Nursing and First Aid Certificates in Abbey Road. The practical nursing I did at the Torbay Hospital and America Lodge. The latter was a temporary home and respite care centre, donated by the Americans for war blinded. I remember many sad cases there; the two Austrian Jewish boys who had been stoned by the Nazis and lost their sight, the old cockney ladies with an unquenchable sense of humour who had been injured in the blitz on London and a young seaman who had been blown up in his first month in the Navy, who was trying to play the piano, in the hope of a career at the end of the war. I shall never forget walking up the driveway to go on duty and hearing the tune "I'll see you again", played hesitantly on the piano.

Just before D-Day, my Commandant, Miss Quant, telephoned me to say that they had lowered the age limit to eighteen and a half and "did I want to go?". By this time I was on the permanent staff of the Prudential Insurance Company, which had been evacuated to Torquay and provided much needed employment to many local women. If I waited until conscription at age nineteen, I would have my pay made up, but I was anxious to join the mobile VADs serving with the Royal

Navy, so there was no doubt about my answer. I was asked to present myself to RNAH Barrow Gurney on the 19th June 1944 and so started one of the most eventful and exciting periods of my life.

Our training proved rather inadequate when we "joined up" and were pitchforked into the duties expected of us on the wards of the Naval Hospitals. I was totally unprepared for the long hours of physical work and the Naval discipline and my time at "Barrow" was not distinguished by any merit on my part. Indeed I was in trouble on three occasions that I can remember, although thanks to our Commandant, Miss Bond, with no lasting blot on my records. My first day on the ward, I enquired of one of the Sick Birth Attendants, the name of the man obviously in charge, "Oh, that's the Killick", he said. I felt it would be rude to address him like that so approached him saying, "Mr Killick". This produced much merriment and I discovered that a Killick was a naval rating, i.e. Leading Hand. My first night duty (they consisted of thirty one nights of twelve hours duration with a snatched half hour on the slats in the linen cupboard, if you were lucky and had a relief between two wards), I remember walking around the forty bedded ward and seeing a number of empty beds - the next thing I remember was the night sister shaking me vigorously. I had apparently climbed up on to one and was fast asleep! It was considered an offence to fall asleep on night duty on one of the ward beds. Oh dear! This was my first experience of nights and twelve hours was a long time and if the ward wasn't busy it was difficult to fight the dreadful drugged feeling of sleep. As time went by, nights became part of life. The next time I was in potential trouble was on the same night duty. Two SBAs had brought down the body of a patient who had died on the Officers' Block above us. They went off for a cup of "char" and I was curious to see what a dead body looked like. He had been rather an unpopular officer who had been feared, but in death he looked strangely vulnerable and I felt terribly sorry for him and doubted whether anyone would mourn him. On impulse, I hurried outside and picked a rose from one of the bushes and tucked it between his hands. I felt as though peace had descended on his body and his soul would rest easy. There was a fearful row next day, it was thought that someone had been less than respecful - I am afraid I didn't own up. I was still happy that I had given him my rose.

In the autumn of 1944, I was on duty on one of the Surgical Wards and most of the patients were up and enjoying the sunshine outside with a game of cricket. There were constant calls for me to go in to bat which I resisted as Matron's and Surgeon Captain's Rounds were due. At last I relented and had just picked up the bat and positioned myself when I looked up to see the full procession. My heart stood still. To be caught by Matron would have been unspeakable, the Surgeon Captain to be with her was 'death' itself. Next morning I was in Miss Bond's office and on draft to Newton Abbot where the old Workhouse had been taken over for the duration.

I wonder if any local people remember the Workhouse as it was? I seem to remember old people talking about the possibility of ending their lives there with dread. One had heard that they separated the couples and were made to wear uniforms. Certainly the wards were forbidding, heated, if I remember correctly, with only a huge stove in the centre of the ward fuelled with coal or coke from large metal coal scuttles. It was an encounter with one of these that placed me in Sick Bay for Christmas 1944. I had a part in the Christmas Pantomine doing a song and dance act with rather an elderly SBA (all of 28 years!). Whilst walking through one of the wards on the inevitable night duty with my nose in the air in response to ribald remarks from the fitter patients, I slipped on the highly polished floor and landed on the edge of the coal scuttle. When I tried to get up I collapsed completely winded and the patients' howls of glee were replaced by cries for help. Result, a week in Sick Bay with a couple

of fractured ribs and my stage debut postponed indefinitely. We seemed to have many more patients there who had been wounded and needed long term care. I remember one night a hospital train had arrived bringing patients, some of whom had come from the Far East. There were visions of a stretcher strewn deck, with one patient who became violent in the night. We also had a number of men who had been released from prisoner of war camps in Europe and it was clear that they were emotionally very fragile. I remember an argument about the General Election which got right out of hand and one patient became very upset. We were in quarters at a house called Yardelands on the hill behind the hospital and the winter of 44-45 was very cold with quite a lot of snow and ice. We had large metal containers for our night duty food, (quite revolting), but we had great fun sliding down the hill to the hospital on the containers!

Whilst I was at Newton Abbot the war in Europe ended and the up-patients and off-duty nurses went "ashore" into Newton Abbot to celebrate. There was a large American Hospital based somewhere near, possibly Stover, and their dances were very popular because of the splendid and bountiful food they laid on (iced cake!!). The rationing for ourselves was still very tight, the Americans brought all their own food in for their personnel and they went short of nothing, so an invite to their dances was such a treat. At midnight my friends and I were dancing around the Clock Tower with some American Medical Personnel to music played by a veteran of the 1st World War. He played his fiddle with great skill and with tears running down his cheeks. There were a number of Foreign drafts coming up, particularly to the Far East and some of my friends went off to Alexandria. I was afraid that I might literally "miss the boat", so asked to go on the very next draft, which happened to be going to Trincomalee, which was then in Ceylon (now Sri Lanka). We had fifteen days leave and I spent part of it going up to London to get my tropical kit. Shortly after returning, the war with the Japanese ended. It was announced at 1 am but we did not hear about it until 7 am, when we got up. Our celebrations were mixed with sadness as we realised how much that war had cost and how many of our friends would never come back. On August 23rd 1945, our draft eventually came through and nine of us were sent to Stonehouse to await our ship to Ceylon.

It wasn't a good welcome. We were sent to quarters at Wingfield, Stoke, where the beds were so damp we slept in our overcoats on top of them. Since we were not expected to stay long, they really didn't know what to do with us, but eventually we were allocated to different wards. From my diary; "We arrived at Plymouth expecting to sail that very day. It seemed a veritable prison and I believe we all hated it - although the nurses were very nice. I remember Sister Milne, LSBA Brown, Dot and Candy and others on the Officers Block!" We finally left on November 17th by train for Liverpool.

The train was absolutely packed with people standing in the compartment and the corridors. I looked longingly at the luggage rack and eventually persuaded some of my friends to help me up there so that I managed to snatch a little sleep on the long journey north. When we arrived at Liverpool we all piled into the Adelphi Hotel for breakfast and a quick clean-up. When we arrived at the docks and found our troopship the "Orduna", she looked incredibly small to me.

R.N.A.S. NEWTON ABBOT.
DEVON.
1944
(Alice Ruttledge)
Sister R. Goodacre,
Q.A.R.N.N.S/R.

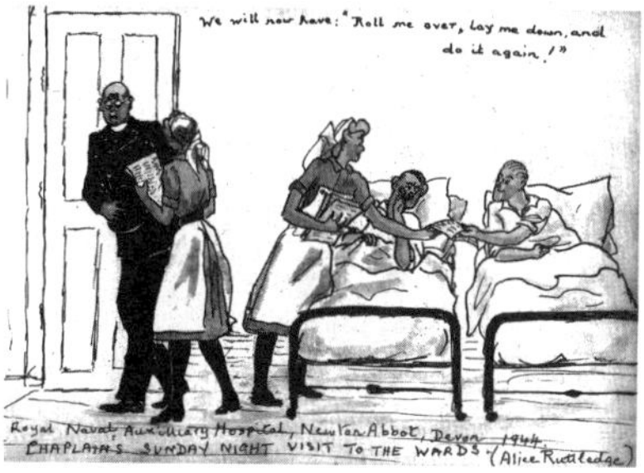
We will now have: "Roll me over, lay me down, and do it again!"
Royal Naval Auxiliary Hospital, Newton Abbot, Devon. 1944.
CHAPLAIN'S SUNDAY NIGHT VISIT TO THE WARDS.
(Alice Ruttledge)

POST OPERATIVE FLAP ~
R.N.A.H. NEWTON ABBOT, DEVON 1945
(Alice Ruttledge)

M.O.s ROUNDS. (E.N.T. Ward)
at R.N.A.H. NEWTON ABBOT
1945.
(Alice Ruttledge)

My candle burns at both ends,
It cannot last the night,
But oh, my friends, and ah my friends,
It sheds a lovely light!
R.N. Auxiliary Hospital
Newton Abbot. 1944
(Alice Ruttledge)

From my diary I see that we were 680 on board including about 200 civilians with many small children and babies. The ship was packed and our cabin had a notice outside to say 'Accommodate 7'. There were 29 nurses packed in and our cabin had three decker bunks, with one's bunk and one nail apiece for all the kit we might need for up to five weeks. There were two wash basins giving water to wash twice a day and ultimately only sea water. For all that, we had a lot of fun and an exciting trip through the Mediterranean and Suez Canal and thence to Aden and India. We left on the 18th November and finally arrived at Colombo on the 19th December, having spent a week offshore at Bombay where we were able to get shore leave and my 20th birthday at Aden where we had a lovely party on the boat deck and the ship's cook baked me a special cake.

We disembarked at Colombo and had to travel overnight to Trinco which was on the other side of the island. The train seemed to be made mainly of wood and had no windows. We ended up sleeping on our kit as whenever the train stopped during the night hands would appear at the window ready to grab anything which wasn't 'tied down'. We had not seen our main luggage from the hold and were anxious that it should not proceed with the ship to Sumatra. We had asked some Naval Officers (including my future husband), who came to see us off, if they could check on it. It did eventually turn up much to our relief. We eventually arrived at the Combined Services Hospital, tired, dirty, to line up before Matron Taylor. She looked at me and barked, "How old are you?". "Twenty, Matron." "Huh! You look about fourteen. They'll be sending me school girls next!". Not a good start, but better than the poor souls who contracted maleria on the way up and were soon on their way home again. We worked hard there, despite the heat up to 120F and the monsoons which could drench you on the way to and from the wards. We worked exactly the same hours as in the UK, although the non-medical male personnel seemed to knock off at midday. I was in the hospital hockey team and we would often play in the heat of the day, but as we played a mixed team against all-men teams our success rate wasn't great. During the time I spent there one of the cruisers came from Singapore with cases of Poliomyelitis on board. They were disembarked to be nursed at the hospital, two of our nurses got the dread disease, luckily not badly, but one got a Disability Pension of 5/- a week. Leaves, rather rare, were spent up in the hills at Diyatalawa or on tea plantations where the planters were very hospitable. Weekend passes were spent at the YWCA, a lovely bungalow on the beach. I remember the choice of breakfast menu, coffee and fruit (paw-paw, mango, plantains) or tea and cooked bacon and eggs. The native village was small and very poor, but you could go to a little shop (straw thatched and rickety) and sketch a dress which would be made up overnight on the most ancient of sewing machines.

Social life was hectic with film shows and cocktail parties on board the ships which came into the harbour and there were dances at the Officers' Club which had an outdoor dance floor. The Marine bands from the ships would play for us. Finally our draft for home came up and eight of us embarked on the Monarch of Bermuda (Shirley Temple's Suite!) on 1st November 1946. It had been a great experience, with moments of sadness when we lost a patient and sometimes one felt homesick and longed

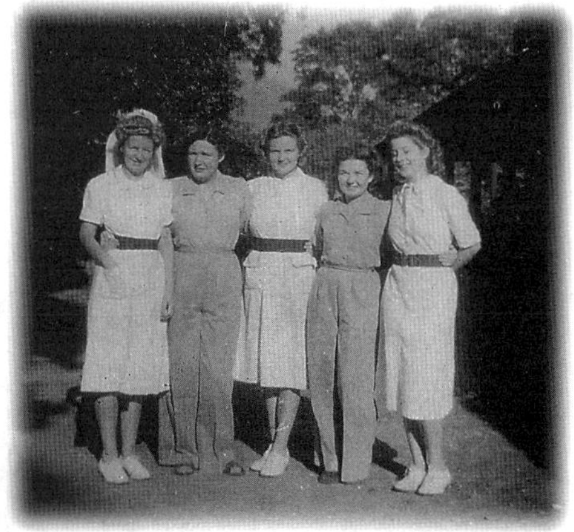

Betty, Chris, Jeannie, self and Diana at Trinco 1945.

for the cliffs and cool air of Devon, but Ceylon was a beautiful island and the people charming and nice looking.

We finally arrived back at Southampton on 19th November, just a year away from home. From my diary; "... first sight of England, with, how did we guess? - a fine drizzle. A miserable sight. We stood on the deck watching the troops disembark and hearing the dockers say, "You'd better go back where you came from!". A Naval working party met us, we went through customs, reported at Haslar and having been issued with railway warrants and what little pay was due to us, left for home at six pm. A friend and I had an awful job getting our kit to the station. We both had large cases, cabin trunks, tin trunks and kit bags and when we arrived at Waterloo, we had real problems. I had "subbed" my pay, and had the magnificent sum of half a crown and my friend had little more. How were we to get to Paddington with all our luggage? I walked out of the station and bumped into an ex-patient, Sergeant West of the Royal Marines. "What's the problem nurse?", he asked. I explained. "No problem", he said, "I'm in charge of transport", and he and his men put all our kit on a lorry and transported us to Paddington, where he bought us a coffee before seeing us on the train. This more than anything else summed up the wonderful spirit that existed in the Services. One could be sure that someone would help out if necessary. I finally arrived home at Torre Station in the early hours of the morning. My family were not expecting me as I had had no opportunity to phone them. I seem to remember leaving my kit at the station and walking home to find everyone in bed. A bit of an anti-climax.

After a fortnight's leave and my 21st birthday spent at home, I returned to Haslar and signed on for a further three months as I had not the remotest idea what to do next. I spent Christmas at Haslar, on duty, and was then posted to Eastleigh which was a Fleet Air Arm Station, finally emerging into Civvy Street at the end of March 1947.

Jessie Muscat Fairchild

Malta took a terrible hammering by the bombers during the war. It was one of our important Naval Bases and it was vital it did not surrender. Anyone who sailed in a Malta convoy will tell you how the enemy regarded the strategic importance of the island, every convoy was harassed by submarines and bombers. It did not surrender. The island was awarded the George Cross which is the highest civilian award. It became 'Malta G.C.'. These are the memoirs of one of her daughters who became an Army VAD.

Joyce Drury

In Remembrance

The brave boys of Britain
and those of Malta too
both fought together
to bring the convoys through.

We all suffered starvation
and many sleepless nights
but it was really worth it
because God was on our side.

We thank the Royal Navy
the Air Force Boys and all
plus the Gallant Regiments
that fought around our shores

We shed tears of sorrow
for the Warriors we had lost
they died for Malta
when all seemed lost.

We are sure they are in Heaven
for their suffering was great
let us pray for 'our Gallant Heroes'
who have passed on through the gate.

by Jessie Muscat Fairchild

Jessie Muscat Fairchild

The 90th General Military Hospital - Imtarfa - Malta 1942

What A Way to Learn!

I can recall many occasions from my time as a VAD at Imtarfa Military Hospital, Malta. One, in particular, I remember with amusement, though at the time I was so embarrassed I would have had no objections if the floor had opened and swallowed me up.

Sergeant Wilson and Corporal Chappel were in charge of ward M2 where I was on duty when a French soldier was brought in. The Sergeant asked me to admit the patient, so following his instructions I helped the Frenchman into a pair of pyjamas and got him comfortably settled in bed. I then proceeded to fill in the necessary forms; his temperature and pulse on his medical chart, his name, address, religion and next of kin on another. Having finished that little job, I turned my attention to sorting out the contents of his kit bag. I had just started to empty it when lo and behold I lost my grip on the handle and all its contents were scattered all over the floor, some items coming to rest under the patient's bed. I noticed Sergeant Wilson standing behind me as I swooped to pick up the contents, including approximately three dozen "finger stalls", or so I thought! I pointed them out to the Sergeant asking, "How many times does he intend to cut his finger?". Much to my bewilderment there was a burst of laughter all around me. Sgt Wilson and Cpl Chappell could not control their fits of hysterical laughter. To say I became very hot under the collar would be putting it mildly. I just could not see the funny side of the "finger stall". As soon as Sgt Wilson could compose himself he put his arm around my shoulders and led me away from the ward to Sister's vacant office where he asked me if I had ever seen something known as a contraceptive and did I know what use it had? Well, having received a negative reply from me, he went on to explain in detail the use of such contraception. I was so very naive. I had not realised what a sheltered upbringing I had had. I really needed to pluck up courage to go back into the ward for it was with great difficulty that I faced the patients, let alone the French gentleman. I had no need to worry, my innocence seemed to have won their affection and they soon made me feel at ease, but I am sure it gave them many a chuckle for a long time afterwards.

In Memory Of Two Brave Boys

When I first enlisted as a VAD at Imtarfa Military Hospital I found nursing very tough as the sight of blood upset me and the terrible sights encountered in a wartime hospital took a lot of getting used to.

I remember vividly the admission to my ward of the crew of a bomber which had crashed and caught fire. I shall never forget the smell of burnt flesh. Two of the boys, Sergeants Smith and Brown, were in very bad shape and we nursed them for many months. Their bodies were covered from head to foot with sterile Vaseline dressings with just a gap over their mouths for feeding. The poor boys looked like Egyptian mummies. Their arms and hands, with the flesh torn and hanging, had to be immersed in sterile saline every day. I used to spoon feed them and attend to their bodily needs.

Slowly and at long last, they improved and the day came when their eyes were to be uncovered. I recall the hush as the whole ward waited with bated breath until they declared that they could see. Then a huge cheer went up.

Eventually the doctors told them that they would be returning to England for skin grafts. We were delighted for them, though sad to see them go because they had won our hearts. Despite terrible suffering, they never lost their sense of humour and we had been happy to care for them.

A week later, to our horror, the hospital received news that their ship had been torpedoed and that Sergeants Smith and Brown had gone down with the ship. It was a terrible shock to patients and staff because we had all grown to love them. To this day I mourn them and they will always live in my memory.

A Demonstration On How To Give A Blanket Bath

The Sister on this special ward was dictatorial but very efficient and a hard worker. On this special morning all was quiet on the ward, so Sister decided to give me the first lesson on how to blanket bath a patient.

Being new on the ward, I was scared of her. I was told to go and fetch a bowl of warm water. In the meantime, Sister had drawn some screens round the patient's bed. As I walked down the ward, a patient called out to me to watch out as the battle-axe was on the warpath. She was ready waiting impatiently for me, her sleeves were rolled up, a rubber apron was wrapped round her waist. She was ready to commence her demonstration.

We first stripped the bed except for a blanket which we kept on the patient then the sister whipped off the patient's trousers and placed them on the radiator. She washed his face, arms and hands, she then turned the sailor on to his side. She gave his back a good wash, dried him and then massaged him with surgical spirit. She then turned him to face me, on doing so she passed the soapy flannel towards me saying, "You can carry on now nurse". Sister stood aside for me to take over. I was very nervous as I had never seen a naked man before. I was embarrassed. To my horror, I dropped the flannel. It landed in between the patient's legs. I hesitated for a moment or two. I eyed the cloth. I was contemplating how I was going to retrieve it when Sister's voice reached me saying, "Come now nurse. Nothing to be afraid of". She suddenly swooped over and grabbed the flannel, gave the patient's private part a rub down and then in a loud voice she remarked, "It won't bite you". A giggle could be heard from behind the screen. Sister then gave me a wink and a smile. I realised that Sister was not a battle-axe but a very human person. From that moment, we became friends.

That morning, we gave four more blanket baths. By the end of the day, I became quite an expert and it was good to see the patients looking so clean and comfortable and they appreciated our day's work.

In the Polio Ward

In 1942, we had a convoy brought into Malta with service men suffering with Polio.

Poliomyelitis is inflammation of the grey matter of the spinal cord. Many patients had complete paralysis, some had congestion of the lungs and had difficulty in breathing. On admittance, some were given lumber puncture.

The nursing staff had to wear gowns, masks and gloves as Polio is very contagious. The ward was full to capacity and extra staff were put on duty as these patients needed a lot of nursing. It was heavy nursing as we had to do a lot of lifting. We had four patients in Iron Lungs. Sometimes we used to get these patients out for a short spell but immediately they had difficulty in breathing, we had to get them back. These boys had to have continual observation.

The hospital had its own generator and it often broke down. Then the orderlies had to work the pumps by hand. It was a very laborious and exhausting but the orderlies were hard working and humane. They were terrific. Many a time they gave up their off duty to help those less fortunate. The nursing staff were a team that would respond to a call of help, day or night, whether they were on duty or not. Sometimes the pumps too broke down. Then the patients had to be given artificial respiration. It was a great trauma for the patients. When the sound of the generator and pumps started up again it was a great relief to the Sister in charge of the ward and especially to the poor patients. Some of the patients were incontinent so they had to be washed often and the bed linen changed and their pressure points dealt with. Some pressure points had to be treated every two hours, also we used to turn the patients on their side and kept on turning them so that they did not develop bedsores. The physiotherapists were kept very busy as most of these boys had to have their limbs exercised. The Sisters and VADs gave a helping hand as well.

Although the patients were so severely handicapped, they still kept cheerful. Some of the lads made progress. Others were not so lucky.

* * *

Social life at Imtarfa was very good. Once or twice a week, dances were held at the Garrison Hall. They were run by the medical officers or other ranks. The female nursing staff attended all these dances. It was fun as we were in great demand. One did not need an introduction, they just came over and asked you for a dance, but often we used to have a Paul-Jones or an Excuse Me dance so everyone had an opportunity to meet with some nice lads. They were very enjoyable evenings. Sometimes we had an ENSA performance or a Cinema show. All up-patients and staff were allowed to attend.

Then we had the dances at the Medina Club which were very popular with the Officers from the three Services. The dances were held by candlelight. Everyone wore evening dress. My regular escort was a Naval Lieutenant. He was on the motor torpedo boats at Manuel Island. He used to come all the way on his motor bike to take me either to the Medina Club or to the Union Club in Valletta. I used to ride pillion in my evening dress down the steep hill of Imtarfa. I found it very exciting. Good thing my father did not know! Parents in those days were strict as they wanted to protect us from men in general. It was embarrassing at times. We were all capable of looking after ourselves.

We also had invitations to units at various Officers' Mess. They provided us with transport. The Queen Alexandra's Sisters used to come with us. They were a friendly lot. Distance was no matter . We were young and we must have been as strong as horses. We were out late at parties and the next day we were on duty doing a long shift. I really don't know how we survived.

Now, in my old age, I often look back with nostalgia for those happy young days.

On Our Way to Italy To Join A Field Hospital

It was early afternoon. We were waiting to board the Troopship Escania. My father had come to see me off. He looked strained and anxious for he feared the ship might be attacked.

The Queen Alexandra's Imperial Military Nursing Sisters and the VADs were ready to board the ship. There was a great feeling of excitement as we walked up the gangway. We sailed out of the Grand Harbour at 6 o'clock with an escort of Destroyers, Mine Sweepers plus an air cover. Even though we were at war, everyone seemed happy. There was a great feeling of togetherness, determination and excitement as we watched Malta disappear from view.

No one went to bed that night, we all stayed on deck. Lifebelts had to be worn at all times. We had a boat drill in case of emergency. Luckily we only needed the rehearsal! The atmosphere on deck, though I would not have thought it possible, grew in intensity as visibility diminished with the coming of night. There must have been hundreds of lookouts that night as we zig-zaged our way behind the Mine Sweepers, for so many eyes were glued to the sea in search of danger. Even our ears strained to hear the sound of enemy aircraft among our own Spitfires zooming overhead.

Next morning brought some relief for the Sicilian coast was now in view which again added to our excitement and as it appeared to grow so did the chatter and laughter. No one had slept yet no one seemed tired. No sooner were our feet on Sicilian soil than they were off again as we crossed from Messina to the Italian mainland. There awaiting us was a convoy of ambulances, trucks and other army vehicles. The doctors, Sisters and VADs travelled in the ambulances and the men in lorries. We had a Military Police escort as we headed for our first posting at a Mobile Field Hospital.

The RAMC vehicles and the ambulance cavalcade was on the move travelling north through Calabria. Our destination was a place called Gravina. To our delight we found along the Auto-strada were miles and miles of olive trees and lovely orchards. The countryside was enchanting. The army drivers made several stops for the members of the party to stretch their legs and to take advantage to answer the call of nature. We all scattered into the fields, the men going in opposite direction to the nurses in search of a secluded place. It was hilarious to see heads popping up from behind scrubs and bushes and to see them all rushing back to join the convoy. The army cooks in the meantime had the primus stoves going and within a matter of minutes served us with hot tea and sandwiches. It was greatly appreciated as we had been on the road for some time. The Military organisation was fantastic. Everything went like clockwork. The journey to Gravina was very pleasant and friendly. We made our destination late afternoon.

The Royal Engineers immediately got down to work. They erected a large marquee which was to be used as an operating theatre and they set up tents to be used as wards. The medical staff were also accommodated in tents. For toilets, the army supplied us with tin huts in which was a bucket, a box of sand and a shovel. It was quite an experience! The next day, the camp was complete and ready to take in casualties.

Off To An ENSA Show

Matron Smith was always ready to organise some outings so this time she arranged to take a group of Sisters and VADs to an ENSA show. She arranged transport and an escort of Military Police. Brindisi was a strong fascist town. The British were their liberators but some Italians were still fanatics and still resented our presence.

We set off with Matron and our Commanding Officer. We were late. The show had already started. Boxes had been reserved for us. During the interval the lights came on. The troops in the Auditorium spotted us. They flashed their torches at us and cheered. I think the boys had not seen any British women around, not since their landing in Italy and the occupation of the Mainland. They were delighted. It took some time before they settled down and then the show went on. It was a good show and we did all enjoy our first night out in Brindisi.

The Fleeing Angels

Brindisi was an old, strong Fascist town. The nursing staff were not allowed out at night unless they had a pass and an armed escort. Part of the town was out of bounds to all British and Allied troops. After three weeks of our movements being restricted, we decided enough was enough and it was time to venture out on our own.

One evening five of us nurses stepped out, for what we thought would be a quiet if not cautious walk to a restaurant. As we came round a corner we spotted the Army Red Caps who were patrolling the streets. We did not hesitate, but as one body we took off, even Mercury would have found it hard to catch us. We sped down cobbled roads and a maze of dark alleyways as fast as our legs could muster. We could hear the sound of heavy boots - panic, they are after us! Some of the locals had noticed us and as we were familiar with the Italian language we asked the 'Eyeties' for a way of escape. They quickly responded to our call for help and joined us in the flight, leading us into a coffee shop and out the back way. We ended up in a spaghetti house, breathless, excited and laughing. It was funny, for the Italian rescuers enjoyed the escapade as much as we did. The owners of the spaghetti house , after hearing what had happened, presented us with a much needed and greatly appreciated large bottle of Chianti! From then on we were known to them as the 'fleeing angels'.

As time went by the 'Eyeties' came to realise that the British were their friends and liberators, from then on things improved and we were able to roam around Brindisi without danger, we no longer needed an army escort. After that we often visited the restaurant, we used to exchange our rations of Woodbine cigarettes for a plate of spaghetti.

Audience With His Holiness Pope Pius XII

His Holiness was giving audience at St Peter's Basilica to members of the British and Allied Forces and wounded men.

The VADs were given an invite, we felt highly privileged to meet the Head of the Roman Catholic Church.

We set off early in the morning for St Peter's. When we arrived we found the Basilica very crowded. We were very lucky, we managed to find a place right by the altar steps. It was a very moving sight to see so many wounded men. They were on stretchers, in wheel chairs, on crutches. It was quite heart rending.

The Pope was carried in shoulder high. Mass was said, Cardinals and Bishops assisted His Holiness in giving Holy Communion. After Mass, His Holiness came down the steps of the altar towards us. As he came forward we went down on our knees. He spoke to each of us VADs. I remember vividly the feeling when I kissed his hand. The emotion was very strong. The Pope spoke to me in French. He thought I was French. When I told him I came from Malta he said a special prayer and then he gave me his blessing. It was a very exciting day for us nurses. We were all very young to have had such an honour. It was a lovely experience and it will last us throughout our lives. It was a memorable day.

On our return to Brindisi and back to our hospital we had a lot to recount to Matron and our friends.

After all these years, it still gives me great pleasure to recollect my memories.

Two Malta VADs On Holiday In Romantic Venice

Carmen and I are off on holiday in Florence.

Miss Margaret Smith our Matron got us our movement orders from our Commanding Officer, Colonel Ervin. Every member of the nursing staff had to apply for a travelling pass before setting off on leave. Carmen and I had our kitbags ready packed, our uniforms cleaned and pressed ready for the following day. That night some of the girls came to our room. We were laughing and chatting away and we did not notice the time go by. It was quite late by the time we got to bed. I could not settle down to sleep. I just tossed and turned and in the end I gave up, I got out of my bed and started to potter about. At 7 o'clock, Carmen and I reported to Matron's office where we collected our travelling permit. Matron shook hands with us and wished us a happy holiday.

Some of the nurses who were off-duty came to see us off at the hospital gate with calls of 'be good - don't do anything that you will later regret, have fun'. It was the usual kind of teasing that goes on amongst young nurses when they get together. Still waving to the girls we got to the end of the road and disappeared from view. We then walked on to the Auto-Strada which was on the outskirts of Brindisi in the hope of getting a lift. Our destination was Bari.

An Army jeep driven by a British soldier came by. We stopped him and asked for a lift. As he was going the same way, he said he would take us. The soldier was very kind and helpful. He drove us straight to Bari aerodrome and to the RAF Information Office. There we parted company thanking him for the lift and he wishing us a happy holiday.

At the RAF Information Office we asked the Officer in charge if there was a flight going to Florence. The reply was 'no'. He saw our faces drop with disappointment. He then suggested we go to the American side of the airport . We did so, this time we struck it lucky. The Americans offered us seats for the following morning, not to Florence but to Venice. We were so delighted that in one voice we cried 'Great!'. I was very tempted to kiss the Officer but I refrained. We kept quiet about not having a permit to Venice. Transport was organised for us to be collected from our hotel.

The next day, after breakfast, two smashing looking blue eyed boys came to pick us up. The two men introduced themselves and then declared that they were going to pilot our plane to Venice. A large American car was waiting for us, we were then driven to the aerodrome. The plane had already re-fueled and was ready to take off. We were quickly ushered on to the plane and within minutes we were airborne. As it was our maiden flight we were invited into the cockpit. The scenery was spectacular. The flight took just over two hours to Venice.

When Venice came in sight it seemed to rise from the water, the beauty of it took your breath way. It was a fantastic sight. The pilot flew low and circled round for us to have a good aerial view of the City. It was a bright sunny day and the beautiful white buildings with their red roof tops stood out, the Gondolas swaying as they were rowed downstream. We flew over the pretty islands scattered across the waters past the domed church of Santa Maria Della Salute and then on to the Lido. The beautiful white buildings with the red roof tops and the deep blue of the Lagoon is still instilled in my memory even after all these years.

As we set foot on the Lido we said our goodbyes to the American pilots and thanked them for going out of their way to make our flight so very enjoyable. As we shook hands they said they would be back for us in a fortnight and would be waiting to take us back to Bari.

The Lido was a fashionable bathing resort with a broad sandy beach. It was a popular place for the British and Allied Forces. There were many hotels and villas with pretty gardens with trellises of Bougainvilla climbers, Hibiscus and many other colourful shrubs. It was a high class residential area. There were rows of shops selling good quality souvenirs. It was a delightful place. After spending some time in the area we hired a Gondola to take us to Piazza San Marco. As both Carmen and I spoke some Italian the Gondolier started to chat us up and then he started singing a seranata. Till then I had hardened my heart against the Italians for bombing my country but Venice and the charm of its people, their language and music had won me over. It was such a romantic, heavenly place. Crossing over from the Lido to Piazza San Marco was delightful.

In Venice we made our way to the RTO (the Railway Transport Officer) and the information and booking office. We produced our Army pass and in no time the official had booked us hotel accommodation. During the War many large hotels were requisitioned by the Army and used by the British and Allied Forces for officers in transit.

The RTO had booked us at the Europa Hotel. The hotel was on the main canal and just round from the famous square, so we did not have far to go. On entering the hotel we were delighted with the magnificient place , the walls, the pillars and floors were all in marble, the decor was exquisite, there were dangling chandeliers everywhere and the ceilings decorated in gilt and paints. The RTO looked after us very well indeed throughout our holiday, as we were put up in lavish accommodation every time.

Our bedroom was large and gorgeously furnished with beautiful antiques and grandiose doorways and paintings. It also had a decorative balcony so we were able to get much pleasure in watching the Gondolas go by. There is always a lot of movement on the canals except on Sundays and public holidays. Most of the mornings we spent being rowed down various canals. We went under the famous Rialto Bridge and the Bridge of Sighs. There are many beautiful palaces along both sides of the Grand Canal. It was very impressive. Some mornings we used to go to the Piazza San Marco. The square is surrounded by dignified buildings under which is an arcade. There is also the Doge's Palace and St Marks Cathedral with its beautiful Dome.

Often we used to sit at the cafes which are set out on the square. It seemed to be a meeting place where young lovers met and where one could have refreshment while an orchestra was playing. It was very relaxing to watch the locals feeding the pigeons. It seemed to be their past time. I was told that the Venetian civil service had a fund to feed the pigeons twice daily.

Carmen Ellul and Jessie Muscat, having a lovely time in romantic Venice.

Carmen and I had a lot of fun walking down Venetian streets which led to little squares and walking over white decorative little bridges which crossed over narrow canals. Some evenings Carmen and I used to go dancing at the Luna hotel which was well attended by British Officers. Some evenings we went to the Daniele for a meal.

After a week in Venice, we decided to venture further north to Triest.

The automobiles do not circulate in the City but are parked immediately on entering Venice. So we made our way to Mestre which is on the outskirts of Venice. From here we hitched all the way to Triest, part of the way in a three ton truck and the rest of the journey in a small Army lorry. In those days it was quite safe for British Nurses to hitch hike on their own for the troops were well disciplined and never took advantage. They were terrific.

Triest was a medium sized town with a lovely promenade all along the harbour. There was a large presence of the British Navy which I loved to see. I always had a soft spot for the boys in the Navy as many of my friends were on the ships and one, a Lieutenant Commander, I had dearly loved and missed.

Again the RTO put us up in the best hotel, the "Internazionale". It was just across the promenade. Our bedroom was large and lavishly furnished. The bathroom had a marble top table with porcelain basin and jug. The marble bath was spacious and enjoyable for one to soak in. Our room had a balcony which faced the harbour. The hotels in Italy always served excellent meals and the vino was delightful.

Three VADs on a day 'off' in 'delightful' Taranto (Italy) on September 18th 1945.

One afternoon we went for a stroll along the promenade when I heard someone call my name. To my surprise I found it was a Royal Naval Commander I had known in Malta. He was very pleased to see us. That evening he took us to a restaurant for a meal. He then phoned for naval transport. The driver was a young sailor , he drove us up a hill. There we had a lovely panorama of Triest by night. We found it beautiful and dazzling with all the lights of the British Naval Ships in the harbour. As it was still very early, the driver drove on. We were climbing up all the time. We found ourselves in mountain passes. We saw pontoon bridges blown up, tanks and lorries on their side and burnt out. There was debris everywhere. We saw large boulders with Tito's name inscribed on them. The Commander told the sailor to turn back for he realised we had lost our way. It was very, very late by the time the driver found his way back to Triest. We all gave a sigh of relief when we reached Triest. The next morning the Commander phoned to tell us that we had strayed into No Man's Land. He said we were very lucky to have got back in one piece. He concluded by saying, "You will have a lot to relate to your children and grandchildren when you grow older".

Our Return to Venice

We again hitched back to Venice and to the Europa Hotel. On arrival we were welcomed by the staff in reception . Our room had been reserved for us. Within minutes of our return a pot of tea was sent up to our room which was greatly appreciated.

Sunday was the last day of our holiday. We woke up early and had breakfast on the terrace. We had to be at the Lido by one o'clock. The Americans were picking us up at the aerodrome to fly us back to Bari. We asked the porter to call us a gondola. After waiting half an hour one turned up. The gondolier rowed us a hundred yards down the Grand Canal when he changed his mind and refused to take us to the Lido. We pleaded with him with no good result instead he started rowing us towards Piazzo San Marco. Luckily an Amphibian craft was making its way towards us. We called out to the Army boys and they came alongside. We asked for their help as we would be in deep trouble with our Commanding Officer if we did not report on duty on the day we were expected back. We were helped out of the gondola into the Duck. The gallant warriors put on speed and away we went. We arrived just in time for our American friends were waiting for us. The Army lads had driven us right up to the tarmac. We thanked them and said our goodbyes. The pilots ushered us on board with the door closing behind us. We waved to the Army lads and then we were airborne. One last lingering glance at Venice and then it disappeared from view.

On landing in Bari we thanked the Americans for their kindness. It was due to them that we had had such an exciting and adventurous holiday. They were absolutely charming. Both Carmen and I felt sad to say goodbye to them as they were terrific.

We had one night in Bari at the Imperiale Hotel. The following day we made our way back to Brindisi to our hospital where we reported to Matron that we were back safe and sound and full of the joys of spring.

Gravina, Italy - Serving with No.1 Mobile Military Hospital 1944-1945

When convoys with wounded men arrived from the Front, all off-duty was cancelled. The nursing staff were at action stations. Within a couple of hours our hospital was full to capacity.

The walking cases arrived first. They were quickly admitted and escorted to the wards. The wounded men were heavy eyed with lack of sleep, their faces lined and sad. Some cried as we helped them to bed. They were exhausted and they just wanted to get off to sleep. We gave them sedatives and dressed their wounds. They were grateful to have us look after them.

The stretcher cases then arrived. There were several severe head injuries and some were in comas. Their uniforms were bloodstained, their head bandages soaked in blood. We could not move them till the Medical Officers examined them. These boys were on the danger list. They were all kept in a separate tent from other patients and on admittance they were given blood transfusion. The VADs and orderlies were appointed to watch over them in case of a change or a sign of rigors.

The Sisters were busy giving Morphine and preparing patients for the Operating Theatre. The Queen Alexandra's Nursing Sisters and doctors were marvellous. They were a great team.

The first days were like a nightmare. Some of the patients were delirious. Those with shellshock used to give piercing screams of terror and pain as they were reliving the battles and the loss of their friends. These boys were continually kept on sedation. They used to cry and had to be comforted like little children till they dropped off into a deep sleep of exhaustion. As days went by some patients died. Others made good progress. It was an immense relief when a badly wounded man came out of a coma. The first sign of a smile was a joy and very rewarding to a nurse.

The war years made me believe in miracles for they did happen in our hospital. When death occurred, your heart cried out for them and it was hard to hold back your tears. It was a jolt to one's system to see such destruction of human beings. I was 22 years old then. To me, the loss of a patient was like losing a member of my own family. It was a terrible impact. These boys were brave young men who fought and died for the love of their country.

Trani - Italy 1944. No.1 Mobile Military Hospital.

The hospital called all medical staff to action stations.

A fleet of ambulances had arrived. This time it was a convoy of Yugoslav Partisans from the mountains of Yugoslavia where they had been hiding and fighting the Germans. In a matter of hours our hospital was full. There were no beds spare. The Yugoslavs had been in the mountains for a long time, medical supplies did not reach them. Some of the wounded had gangrene set in. The Partisan doctors had no option but to operate and amputate without giving anaesthetic.

As we admitted them, the patients were stripped, their clothes were put in an incinerator, their heads were shaved, those that could walk were taken to shower, the rest were taken to the wards where they were given a blanket bath. As we removed their dirty, saturated dressings we found some of the wounds covered in maggots. We were told some time later by a surgeon that the maggots had helped the healing of some of the wounds. *(It may be interesting to note that modern day trials have shown maggots to be the most effective treatment for wounds, requiring no anaesthetic and leaving less scaring than conventional surgery).* Many of the Yugoslavs had no limbs and some had facial disfigurement. I recollect one lad had his nose and part of his face shot off. He also lost his sight. His jaw was broken so he had to have his teeth and jaw wired up. A length of rubber tubing was inserted in between his teeth so that the patient would be able to suck up nourishing drinks. For many weeks he was on liquids. One day he went into a kind of fit. He could not stand the hunger. He tore his hair and pulled all the wired teeth and jaw apart. He then broke down and cried. He was then taken to the theatre to have his jaw rewired. His face had to be treated every three hours. He had a deep hole where his nose used to be. I had to syringe it with Eusol or sterile saline water. As the hole granulated the wound started to close up. Often I had to use a silver nitrate pencil to level the skin. This boy went through a lot of suffering. He was an excellent patient and a very brave one. Months later he was transferred to a British hospital where they specialised in skin graft.

The Yugoslav Partisans were a happy lot. They put pictures of Tito on the walls. They sang folksongs and hailed Tito. Most of them had lovely baritone voices.

Some were extremely good looking. All were very polite and courteous. Few spoke English. Their captain, Nicola Rabatic, acted as their interpreter. The day the Yugoslavs were departing from our hospital to a general military hospital, Captain Nicola Rabatic made me stand in the middle of the ward. He then read out a letter which was written in French. It was on behalf of his men to thank me and all the nurses that had looked after them. One by one the Partisans came over and shook hands with me and then walked out of the ward. The Captain was the last one to go. He gave me a kiss on each cheek, handed me the thank you letter and departed. We were sorry to see them go because they were a great lot and had suffered so much under the Germans. I presented the letter to the Malta war museum.

Delightful Memories of a Holiday in Rome - 1945

The VAD Commandant, Miss Margaret Briffa, the Noble Helen Testaferrata, the Noble Maud Sant Cassia and I made our way to Brindisi railway station. An Army Transport Officer met us at the gate of the station and escorted us on to the train for Naples. The train was crowded with Italians, British and Allied Forces. A coach had been reserved for us. We were travelling third class. The first and second class had been confiscated by the Germans. The seating in the coach was a long wooden bench which was most uncomfortable for a long journey. An armed guard stood outside the door of our compartment to prevent the Italians chatting us up. The train's departure from Brindisi was late afternoon. It was bitterly cold and it was snowing heavily. Some of us had not seen mountains or snow before. It was so beautiful and picturesque that we spent most of the night with our eyes glued to the windows. We were so very thrilled with it all. The train made several stops at little stations to take on water. Some stations were quite noisy with young Italian boys clamouring on to the train to sell bottles of vino. It was quite fascinating to hear different dialects spoken. Some of the Eyeties were begging for cigarettes and chocolate. We gave them our ration of woodbines and some biscuits. The British soldiers were half hanging out of the windows to hand out some of their rations and money. In Calabria, southern Italy, there was a lot of poverty and hunger that the young girls were selling themselves for food. There was a lot of hardship and disease. Many places were out of bounds to all British and Allied troops due to venereal disease being rampant.

It was very enjoyable on the steam train. The night seemed to pass very quickly. Some of the service boys started singing popular tunes and as the train chugged away the tunes were picked up further down the train. It was an unforgettable night.

We made Naples at 7 o'clock. As we got to the station, a railway Army Transport Officer met us. He introduced himself and then he drove us to the Officers' Mess which was up on a hill. I believe the place was called the Vomero. We were served with breakfast and then we were taken on a tour round Naples and on to Pompeii and Vesuvius. After the tour we were taken back to the Mess for tea.

Late afternoon, we returned to the railway station to catch a train for Rome.

All our accommodation was booked in advance by our Matron, Miss Margaret Smith and our Commanding Officer of our hospital, "Colonel Ervin". It was marvellous how the Army looked after us nurses. We were always treated like officers.

On arrival in Rome we made our way to the Victoria Hotel which was close to the shopping centre. We reported to reception, signed in then a porter took charge of our luggage and he showed us to our rooms. We had a quick shower and unpacked and then we went down for breakfast. Soon after we dashed out of the hotel and we hired a Carrozzella. We all squeezed in. It was great fun. We were young and ready for adventure and we had the same interests and sense of humour. During our stay in Rome we put in as much sight-seeing as we could. Rome is a beautiful city. Its sculpture of the Victorio Emanuele Monument and the fountains with their Statuettes were exquisite. The paintings in the Vatican and in the Sistine Chapel were priceless and we were thrilled with St Peter's Basilica.

We had worn our shoes out we did so much walking. One of our favourite walks was down Via Venito to the elegant little shops and then on to Via Del Trittone right down to Via Imperiale to the Coliseum. Often we used to visit cafes and sit and watch the world go round.

When War Came To An End

The church bells were ringing. The din was terrific. People in the street were cheering. I remember all off-duty was cancelled, we were all on duty on the wards. Matron and our Commanding Officers, Doctors and Sisters joined us. There were plenty of drinks and food going round. Matron was dishing it out. Everyone was kissing and some were in tears. The patients and all the staff had a wonderful time and we all thanked God that the horrible war was over.

The Army taught us a lot of things like discipline, caring, coping with life, independancies and love for others.

While in the Army we were lavished with presents from patients and on occasion a proposal of marriage.

The men in the three services were a great lot. God bless them. It was a privilege to have looked after so many brave men.

After her war service, Jessie lived in Scotland for six months with her sister who was married. She then went to the Sudan on holiday with her sister and brother-in-law who was working for 14 months there. While in the Sudan she met her English husband, from Lincolnshire. They married in 1949 and stayed in the Sudan until 1969. They then came back and settled in England with their four children. Sadly her husband died in 1971.

Hazel Gatherer nee Dobson

Hazel Gatherer nee Dobson was there at the opening of Stoke Mandeville in 1941 and then, having moved to Plymouth to be in the heavy raids of 1941 when she had to run for her life, she went onto HMS Daedallus where she had a very frightening experience with an escaped Italian prisoner of war. These are her memoirs.

Joyce Drury

Waiting to be called up, I enlisted in the National Hospital Nursing Reserve. I joined the RNVADs in 1941 and was sent to Stoke Manderville, which we opened. When I read about it in these days it is very nice to know I was there at the beginning of such an important hospital. After eight months I was drafted to RNH Stonehouse, Plymouth in time for those dreadful air raids of 1941.

Taken at HMS Daedalus II - after Plymouth

Our hostel suffered a direct hit and was destroyed. We fled out of the burning building, but where to go? The tar on the roads was on fire, we were surrounded by smoke which made it difficult to see. We eventually reached the Citadel on Plymouth Hoe where the soldiers took us in. They put us in the underground bunker until next morning when we picked our way through the burning city to RNH Plymouth. We had only underclothes, overcoats and our gas masks. The Doctors' wives and the Sisters at RNH were very good and rummaged around and found us all clothes of sorts to wear. (My photograph at the beginning of my memoirs shows my Red Cross dress fraternizing with my St John apron. My pride and joy was a pair of (extremely large) orange fleecy lined bloomers which fell down around my ankles in the ward!)

Matron at RNH had heard that we were all killed. She received us with tears of delight in her eyes when we all arrived next day. She transferred three patients out of H2 ward and made us get into their beds for a sleep whilst clothes were found for us. I remember I was given a London Hospital outfit down to my ankles. We continued working on the wards then they decided we needed a

RNH Plymouth 1941, **Hazel after second night of Plymouth blitz. Lost all clothes and uniforms.** *'The Captain's daughter loaned me these odd bits to wear. Just after this was taken, a bomb destroyed this building - my ward E2 and E3. Two killed, 'Bunny' Williams SBA and a patient.'*

Miss Bennett, our Commandant, on balcony outside I Block, our home after being made hostel-less.

break from the bombing so they drafted some of us to Maristow which was out in the country away from the raids. I enjoyed my stay at Maristow. It had a feeling of forgotten time dating back to the 14th century. While there, the nurses and SBAs gave the patients a treat. We quietly arranged a little concert in the church at midnight. L/SBA Salmon played the organ and VAD Wilkinson (Wilkie), who had a voice like Isobel Bailey, sang. The church walls were thick and sound proof so no one heard until someone came in and left the door ajar so sound and light came through. Warrant Ward Master doing his rounds noticed it! He swept into the church and closed it all down, which was rather sad because everyone was enjoying this pleasant interlude. We didn't get into trouble but I think the patients were reprimanded. That Warrant WM was a hard and unfeeling man.

We worked hard on the wards but like all young people we liked to play.

Back view of Maristow House. Our mess room is the nearest bay window to tower. Chapel extreme right attached to house.

There had been many stories about the Tower, it was thought to be haunted because strange noises came from it. One day they dared me to climb up the Tower, so with a few inner tremors, I climbed. Would there be some 'presence' when I got there? There was! An owl's nest with baby owls making all sorts of strange noises.

After a few months I went back to RNH for a short stay before being drafted on this time to HMS Daedallus, where many things happened to me.

Maristow Ship's Cat

One of the patients, a Leading Wren, had been very ill. She awoke from a deep sleep and said that she would love some mushrooms on toast. "Would you really? Well, I'll get you some, don't move a finger 'til I get back".

I ran down to the field and was filling my apron with mushrooms when I felt a gun on my shoulder. Slowly I got up and the gun was stuck in my chest. A lifetime past in my mind. I thought I was about to die. It was an escaped Italian prisoner of war. What to do? I gave the most charming smile I possessed and gently pushed the gun away. He pointed to the woods and in sign language asked me to go. I signed that I had to take the mushrooms back first! Still giving a brilliant smile, but my heart was trembling inside, would he shoot me as I turned on my heel and walked back to the ward? I made myself walk at a normal pace then when I got near enough I ran. The guard turned out and caught him. I gave my patient her mushrooms on toast then sat very quiet for a little while to get over the trauma of my meeting with the prisoner.

Maristow Tower **'Digging for Victory',**
'From yonder ivy mantled tower,
The moping owl doth to the moon complain,
of such as wandering near her secret tower,
Molest her ancient, solitary reign.'

The WRNS 3rd Officer and I befriended an old lady who lived in a cottage nearby. She kept lovely pigeons. One day we cleaned their loft out for her. The old lady said that as a little present I could choose any book from her bookcase. I didn't need any reward for helping her but to please her I took one. I opted for a book of poems by Milton. A few lines of which have always stayed with me:

'The mind is its own place,
It can make a heaven of hell
or a hell of heaven.'

One of the men came for us. They had found her lying in her drive. Sadly she had died. The only good thing was she had gone suddenly, an independent soul like her would not have enjoyed life having to be taken care of by someone else.

A L/Wren was brought into the sick bay and admitted. The MO thought she was too sick to be moved to hospital. The Sister was on weekend leave so I had to nurse her around the clock. As there was no bell in the ward to my quarters I decided I must sleep the night on the ward. It was good that I did, she awoke in the night in violent pain. I called the MO. With great care the patient was transferred to hospital. Monday came, the Sister returned and gave me a very hard time because I had slept in the ward. It was against the rules. It didn't matter that the poor girl might have died if I had not bent the rules. She was going to have me reported for this. First she took me before the MO, Doctor Bather. As I left his office he gave me a sly wink. Next thing I knew Sister was on draft and I had been promoted to Supervising VAD.

I was demobbed from RNH Plymouth in 1946. When I left the RN, I was given SEN (State Enrolled Nurse) automatically, a terrible waste of nursing power. I discovered that civilian SRNs just didn't believe what we had done and were capable of.

I married in 1949 but sadly my husband died in 1969.

I still remember my time as an RNVAD with so many happy memories.

This verse was written by the patients in Ward Three, Maristow and given to me in an autograph album when I left. My most treasured possession.

The (Sincere) Lament of a Matelot

I never 'ad much use for poems,
They allus seemed 'goofy' ter me,
An yet, when I thinks
Of the eats and the drinks
An' the care us all 'ad in Ward Three.

From "Dobbie" ('er what is called "Angel")
An' by crikey! that's jest what 'er is)
I feel it's jest time,
To tell 'er in rime
Jest 'ow much us'll miss 'er old "phiz"

An' the smile what never was missing
Whenever 'er come through the door
An' the laughs an' the jokes
What 'er 'ad wi' us mokes
Even while us was askin' for more

Of the care an' attention 'er give us,
Wi' never a grunt or a moan
Of the tea that us supped,
An' the gash that us copped
Up, at dinner. Jest like bein' 'ome.

So say us "God Bless" an' "Good Sailin'"
An' may 'er lifes' v'yage be fair
An lets 'ope we'll see 'er
To toast 'er in beer
Or in water if nowt else is theer

(Signed: A Edkins/F George/W Walker/J Power/R Strickland/R Kine "Glamour Boy" & Paddy)

0800

EXIT – NIGHT STAFF!
OFFICER'S BLOCK,
ROYAL NAVAL HOSPITAL,
PLYMOUTH

1944

Alice Ruttledge.

PLYMOUTH 1944

Alice Ruttledge

Eye treatments,
C2 Ward. ROYAL NAVAL HOSPITAL, PLYMOUTH, 1944
Alice Ruttledge

Officer's Block,
R.N. Hospital,
Plymouth
1944
"You can come out now,
Mr Gordon!"
Alice Ruttledge.

Officer's Block,
R.N. Hospital
Plymouth.
1944
BLACKOUT. (Alice Ruttledge)

Margaret Wood nee Bailey

This is one of our Scottish VADs who went to Australia and married an Australian. Margaret writes an interesting article and has sent interesting memorabilia from Australia.

Joyce Drury

Margaret Wood (nee Baillee) RNVAD 694069 (1942).

I had survived the London Blitz, seventy six nights of continuous air raids from dusk till dawn, had often slept in tube stations, yet was never scared, only angry. Angry that my progressive and chosen career had been affected. It seems so long ago now; we were young, patriotic and fanatically dedicated to the war effort, and my contribution was to nursing. And now, here I was, dead scared, attached to the Royal Navy as a mobile VAD, a mobility that was to take me to Australia . . . forever.

For someone who had always valued privacy, my introduction to communal living was traumatic. I was marched into a cold, brick building of 24 cubicles, two nurses to each. The only heating was a coke combustion stove half way down the passage, totally inadequate in a Scottish winter but a comfortable haven for walkabout rats in summer. Left alone to unpack my now restricted wardrobe, I tried to minimise the obvious restrictions of my new life with its austere environment. I looked around for signs that would identify my room mate, but the only article of clothing for inspection, without trespassing, was an enormous pair of service issue knickers, strung out of sight behind the dressing table. I despaired, not at the proportions of my room mate, but they looked as though they also served as a duster. What had I done! While thus indulging in self doubts, my room mate came off duty and I was pleasantly surprised by her scrubbed up appearance, not in keeping with the dusty old knickers. Without hesitation she removed the knickers and started to dust. I exploded and told her what I had thought. The ice was broken. She proved an ideal companion; considerate, in fact entirely predictable. She showered around 9 pm; read for half an hour exactly, and very early in our association, I learned to close my ears as she plopped her dentures into a tumbler beside her bed.

But let me tell you about my first day in the ward. I endeavoured to look as though it was an everyday occurrence for me to find twenty-four sailors sitting up in bed to attention, like a guard of honour. Twenty-four pairs of eyes drilled through me while my vital statistics were assessed aloud and that the new nurse was bandy to port. "What does that mean?", I gathered the courage to ask. When the laughing died down I was informed that my left leg was slightly bow. I have never been in doubt since about the starboard and port side of a ship. I coped with urgent requests for bed pans but only when I had run out of screens did the Sister appear and inform them that the fun with the new nurse was over and would all up-patients get up. All leapt out of bed! I thought that first day would never end and when I crawled on to the hard, unyielding hospital bed, my feet throbbed as if they would fall off. However, that was the first day of four wonderful years of hard work, some tears, lots of laughter, fun in unfunny situations - a complete medley of emotions but never, never any regrets.

I nursed in several hospitals in Scotland before being drafted to Australia. I acquired new values, a new tolerance of people as individuals and when promoted to Senior VAD had the rare luxury of a room to myself with an unshared wardrobe and a chair! Rationing of food was strict and unrelenting. I traded my cigarette coupons for sweet coupons which enable me to send sweets home. Civilians were not as fortunate as we were for they had nothing to swap. We 'for the duration nurses' became regular Robin Hoods - for 'the boys'! I could fill a book with experiences and memories, memories I love to conjure up and do. And here I am now, three children and ten grandchildren later, remembering the way we were!

Members of British Naval VAD, Margaret is the VAD bending down, top of ladder. She would love if one of the girls here would contact her.

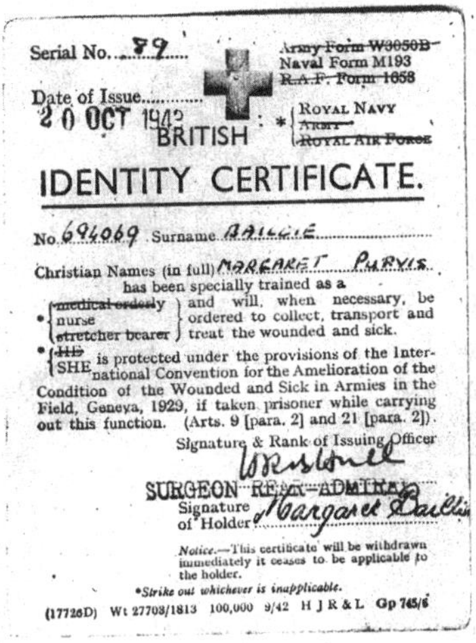

Serial No. 79

~~Army Form W3050B~~
Naval Form M193
~~R.A.F. Form 1658~~

Date of Issue 20 OCT 1942

BRITISH

* ROYAL NAVY
~~ARMY~~
~~ROYAL AIR FORCE~~

IDENTITY CERTIFICATE.

No. 694069 Surname BAILLIE

Christian Names (in full) MARGARET PURVIS

has been specially trained as a
* ~~medical orderly~~ / nurse / ~~stretcher bearer~~ and will, when necessary, be ordered to collect, transport and treat the wounded and sick.

* ~~HE~~ / SHE is protected under the provisions of the International Convention for the Amelioration of the Condition of the Wounded and Sick in Armies in the Field, Geneva, 1929, if taken prisoner while carrying out this function. (Arts. 9 [para. 2] and 21 [para. 2]).

Signature & Rank of Issuing Officer

SURGEON ~~REAR-ADMIRAL~~

Signature of Holder Margaret Baillie

Notice.—This certificate will be withdrawn immediately it ceases to be applicable to the holder.

**Strike out whichever is inapplicable.*

(17726D) Wt 27703/1813 100,000 9/42 H J R & L Gp 745/6

The paybook and identity which we all had to carry and present on demand.

These cases cost us £1.25 each, never wore out. Were made to go in ship's hold. I still have two 'Navy' cases.

Marcelle Dawson nee Grennan

Marcelle has done some drawings of uniforms which we have included in this book.

Drawing by Marcelle Dawson nee Grennan.

In November 1943, twenty-eight VADs met at Liverpool to join a convoy sailing to the Far East. We arrived at the Liverpool docks and after a long walk found our ship, the Reina del Pacifico. It was already full of passengers, mostly in khaki, lining the decks and shouting encouragement to us as we approached. We set sail the next day, slipping away from our berth with just a few dockyard workers to wave 'good-bye' and wish us luck. For a long time we sailed West and thought we may be going to America but were told we had been avoiding a submarine. We were the second convoy to use the Mediterranean since it had been closed and a complete blackout was being observed. We were just able to see the rock of Gibraltar as we slipped by at night.

One morning, several of us who were early risers were walking on deck when we saw something coming up out of the sea. To our horror we saw it was a conning tower. For a moment we were rooted to the spot but the conning tower opened and out came a RN sailor followed by a Naval Lieutenant. We shouted 'good morning' to each other and they climbed back in and disappeared. It was almost disappointing but I do not know what we would have done had it been a German submarine.

There were many troops on board, most of them bound for Burma or stations in India. We VADs spend hours altering tropical kit for some of our fellow passengers and, one afternoon, whilst we were doing this our convoy was suddenly attacked by Stukas diving out of the sky. The klaxons were sounded and covers were ripped off the guns, men were rushing to action stations and bombs were sending great jets of water up in the sea. Someone threw a blanket over my head and pushed me below deck. We were told to go to our cabins, prepare for possible evacuation and have all necessary documents on us. We thought of all the troops below the water line and worried for them. These attacks were repeated for a few days only to be followed by threat of German E-boats.

Our convoy escorted us to the Suez Canal and stood by as we sailed past them. The men on their decks cheered and waved as we shouted 'Thank you' and 'Safe journey'. We were now out of danger. There were many Army camps in the desert alongside the Canal and the soldiers shouted greetings and told us we were going the wrong way! At Aden the RAF band came aboard and gave us a concert. Our new escort was the Royal Indian Navy which included an aircraft carrier for planes for anti-submarine patrols. It was particularly exciting to sail into Bombay harbour, the gateway to the East. We stayed there a few days and were able to go ashore but slept on board. The Commando troops had to deal with our luggage, a hot and tiring job so we organised dozens of jugs of cold lemonade. After a few exciting days in Bombay we boarded a train for Madras, sleeping in comfortable bunks at night whilst all the soldiers aboard had to sleep in their compartments with little or no comfort; a condition which we all resented. At Madras it was Christmas Day and we were taken in small groups to the beautiful homes of senior Civil Servants and business men. Cool beds waited so that we could rest and luxurious baths were there with loose robes to wear while our uniforms were washed and dried in time for Christmas dinner. We all met at the Governor's residence in the evening for drinks and then boarded the train taking us to the coast where we were to board a boat for Ceylon. It was now dark and the train was in the charge of a drunken Australian soldier and was the most frightening journey I have ever taken. We were all glad to transfer to the small, uncomfortable boat to Ceylon arriving hours later, dirty and exhausted at The Hermitage, Colombo, our new home, clean, cool and welcoming.

Drawing by Marcelle Dawson nee Grennan.

The war in the Pacific resulted in many injured being brought to the RN hospital in Colombo. Amongst the most distressing were the 'burns' casualties. I was haunted for many weeks after nursing a sailor who had multiple burns to his body. His ship had been sunk and he was immersed in oil covered water which had caught fire. There was little one could do for him as his whole body had been affected. He was being nursed in a saline bath which must have been painfully uncomfortable for him and he begged us take him out. This was quite impossible and there was nothing one could do but talk to him and try to keep his mind occupied, a vain and hopeless task. That afternoon, whilst I was off duty, he died. I thanked God but it took many weeks to overcome the horror of that poor lad's suffering. I still remember him quite clearly.

In Ceylon there was always the possibility of invasion. One evening a lone Japanese plane was sighted and sirens were sounded. There was a mass evacuation of the native population. The trains had passengers on the roof as well as hanging on to the sides! Nothing happened but many were back before morning. We were given 'Geneva Cross' armbands to wear in the event of a Japanese invasion but were always rather doubtful of the protection that would afford.

It was in Colombo that we had our first case of poliomyelitis in the Doris Beale Hospital for women. The young Wren was desperately ill and in such pain that she wanted to die. Nevertheless she fought in spite of many drawbacks and had a wonderful sense of humour. An iron lung was flown down, I believe, from Trincomalee and until then she had been depending on physiotherapy and oxygen. She was paralysed from the waist down permanently but was a real fighter and had a great sense of humour. We missed her when she was flown back to the UK. Many years later I saw her photograph on the cover of the Picture Post. She was at a rehabilitation centre and I wrote to her there. She had married and, against Doctor's orders, had two sons and lived in a super bungalow. I visited her and we recalled her days of pain and frustration. She also visited me, driving herself and sons in a specially adapted motor car.

It was in Colombo that we had a case of small pox. The patient was one of our staff, due to be returning to the UK in the near future. At first he had been suspected of having Denghi fever but his fever was high and I was put on 'special' watch overnight. During the night the unmistakable rash erupted and he became very ill. He begged not to go to the isolation hospital but there was no option and he died there a few days later. I was isolated for some time too and it was a rather worrying time.

I left Ceylon in 1946 and the Royal Navy later the same year with so many happy memories.

Joy Turner nee Felks

Joy Turner is the Chairman of the VAD (RN) Association. She has written about her experiences while at RNH Chatham.

Joyce Drury

I was at school at Latymor Grammar School in North London when the War broke out.

I joined the Red Cross as soon as I was allowed after working for First Aid and Home Nursing Certificates and undergoing Anti-gas and ARP training, did duties at the local cinema, nursing homes also the First Aid Post at the North Middlesex Hospital.

Joy in the Red Cross 1942, Middlesex 356 Detachment.

I shall always remember the night phosphorus bombs were dropped and several firemen from Edmonton got phosphorus burns on their hands and faces. We Red Cross people were asked to go to the casualty area at the main hospital as we knew how to treat this gas. The firemen were very tired from long hours of duty and they were so brave when their burns burst into flames once they were dry and we scraped the phosphorus with wooden spatulas underwater.

At last I felt useful! I worked my "hours" on the wards of the North Middlesex Hospital, I'd decided to join the Navy as a mobile VAD. Our Commandant of the Middlesex 356 Detachment, Mrs Hamilton, was a lovely lady - an excellent first aider who was an Industrial Nurse at British Oxygen Co.; she gave we three who had decided to go mobile an excellent grounding as Red Cross nurses.

My calling-up papers took me to Barrow Gurney five days before Christmas. It was the first time I'd left home, I felt very lonely and a little miserable at Christmas. I'd had a load of vaccinations and injections, it was snowing, altogether, I was feeling a bit low. I was "specialling" a man found in a hangar in Italy who had such severe gangrene (legs, back and arms) that he had to be nursed face downwards and his dressings done four hourly. His dear little wife sat patiently beside the bed in the single cabin which had a disgusting smell from the rotten flesh which we tried in vain to mask with disinfectants. Our patient died in the New Year.

In due course, I was posted to Chatham and Margery Welsh from my home town was posted with me. We both felt more confident now that we knew the Naval expressions and routine, and went happily to Kent. The VAD Mess members made us welcome, but I was surprised to see we were in tunnel type quarters (like an enormous Anderson shelter was my first impression). I liked the layout of the RNH Chatham, with its large lawned Quarter-deck, surrounded by buildings, and a chapel which I found very peaceful. Everywhere looked well cared for and I was happy on the wards but we were told we were only there until arrangements could be made to move us to the Southern Hospital, Dartford which had been taken over almost completely for service personnel.

At Dartford, I worked on Block D, all RN patients, but with a civilian Sister-in-charge, a Sister Durrant, and some nurses in training. Sister was exceptionally nice to we VADs and one could learn so much from her. She organised the Chief PO (patient) to encourage up-patients to help us and everyone worked hard, wanting to please her. She thought it so funny when she complimented a sailor on the excellent way he polished the ward floor. "You mean how I bumper the deck Sister" he said. After that she always asked the Chief PO, who at that time was a submariner called CPO Bussey, who was bumping the deck that day. A lovely lady, who made me think that perhaps I should take my training and become a State Registered Nurse. After a while on day duty, I then did a night duty on D Block. The food we took on to the wards with us was disgusting. The basket we collected was the type Little Red Riding Hood carried on the way to visit her grandmother, but the contents would not even have pleased the wolf!

In the single cabin was an RN Padre, who was not liked by the patients (or indeed the staff). He is the only Rev. I ever met in the Navy who was sanctimonious and unappreciated by those serving in his area.

VE Day dawned during my time at the Southern Hospital and the excitement was great! The hospital was next to a hospital for nervous diseases and as therapy the patients there grew lots of vegetables. The Doctors, physiotherapists and nursing staff managed to "scrump" some of these vegetables and we concocted an enormous vegetable soup/stew in the Doctors' bungalow, whilst others went searching for old branches and anything suitable to make an enormous bonfire. The hot soup was great - we always seemed to be hungry as food was still rationed and we sang round the fire, and up-patients joined us in celebrating Victory in Europe. There was only one complaint - from the Padre patient in D Block!

I was sent for just after VE Day to report to the Naval Office, where I was told I was to proceed on Embarkation Leave as I was to go to the Far East (where we were still at war!). I went to Chatham for my orders and was sent on leave with a rail warrant to return to RNH Chatham for embarkation - most of which was spent rushing around buying the tropical uniform required - white dresses, white shoes, mess kit, evening dress etc.

Back at Chatham, I was told that the draft had been delayed, and we were to work on the wards. I was very fortunate because two of us were asked if we were prepared to work in the Zymotic (infectious) block. Apparently the Surgeon-Captain had decided the morale of the TB patients was low and the RN "Schoolie" and the Occupational Therapist said that they were finding it difficult to encourage the men to take an interest in anything constructive. We were told that they (the TB patients) felt the war was over, but for them the days were longer and more depressing. We two VADs were asked to help in this "morale boosting" exercise; we both found the work rewarding and hoped that we encouraged the patients to find life more interesting. We found some could sketch, or paint, and Sister allowed us to fix these to the screens, others tried to do crosswords invented by others (full of Naval terms and, I fear, some disrespectful clues!). Two men with artificial pneumothorax yearned for black pudding and I was able to queue for this at a "ration-free" offal shop in Gillingham.

During this time, I attended the little Church in the hospital grounds that I had liked so much on my previous posting to Chatham and started Confirmation classes. With the war starting I had somehow missed out on this (much to my parent's sorrow as they met at their confirmation by the Bishop of Willesden in 1912). I attended the classes in the Padre's cabin with Doctors, Sisters and SBAs and we were all confirmed in Rochester Cathedral by Bishop Chevasse. (He was an ex-service Padre who had lost his legs in battle, so was very impressive as we Naval types took our first communion). We all had tea together afterwards in a little cafe on the corner, near the Cathedral, before getting the "Liberty ship" (an old RN bus!) back to RNH.

It was in Chatham Post Office when I was buying stamps wearing my outdoor Red Cross uniform with my home detachment "Middlesex 356" on the shoulder that I had a laugh. Some Americans were trying to work out which service I was in. One came and read my shoulder and called to his friends, "Look at this, she ain't a dame and she ain't a guy - she's a Middle-sex". Everyone in the post office started grinning and I could feel myself blushing.

I found Chatham town an exciting place to be, as it was service orientated. The Surgeon Rear-Admiral at RNH was a much admired man, who walked occasionally with a stick, not to assist his gait, we decided, but to shake at people who put a toe on the quarter-deck, or to indicate his disapproval of anyone improperly dressed or any of the Sick Berth staff who didn't salute smartly. When I met him at a wardroom drinks party, I was quite surprised at how sociable and charming he could be.

The day came when five of us were informed that our posting had come through - to Trincomalee in Ceylon. The other four going with me were Barbara Egerton, Pam Byass, Sheila Heaps and Margery Welsh. The VAD who saw to our mess catering made a special pudding for us the night before we left - it was called "Banana Mousse". We hadn't seen a banana since we were children (bananas had to be brought on ships, convoys were too precious to use on luxuries, only essential goods came as cargo) and wondered how this special dessert had been concocted. We found out that this wonderful girl had discovered she could get synthetic banana flavoured essence and had used this to mix with mashed turnips and a little of the brown sugar ration - in the RN we were given brown sugar for our tea or anything we needed to add sugar to. (It tasted fine at the time). We were told that there were five rolls in the oven ready for us to warm up for our breakfast, and advised not to eat them cold as they were a bit stale. Our alarm clocks weren't needed as we were awake most of the night doing last minute packing and scribbling letters to our nearest and dearest. We had to be ready very early for the "Liberty Ship" to take us to the Railway Station, so the oven was switched on and the kettle put on to boil. Unfortunately the rolls got overcooked and when we sat with a slightly blackened roll and margarine, with a cup of tea with powdered milk each, we wondered if it was the sort of meal one should have to start a journey of several hundred miles and it was a hilarious start to our journey from Kent to the Far East!

We went to Trincomalee, sailing from Liverpool on the Orduna - but that is another story.

1943 Walking-Out Uniform.

Dorothy Lewes nee Jacob

Dorothy Lewes, who was 86 years old, spoke to me and gave me permission to use her memoirs saying, 'I hope this is going to come out soon because I want to read it before I die.' She unfortunately died in October 1994, but I am sure she will read it in the spirit world.

Joyce Drury

On 13th January 1942, a complete Naval Hospital unit sailed from Glasgow in the largest convoy ever, to take over Colombo General Hospital. I was one of the thirty five VADs in the party. Our incredible voyage ended on 10th March 1942 when we disembarked in Colombo Harbour in torrential rain. A few days later, Colombo and Trincomalee were attacked in two audacious raids by Japanese aircraft, catching a complacent set-up unawares and completely unprepared. Several ships in Colombo harbour were hit and casualties were heavy. One civilian was killed on the Galle Face Green. Suicide 'Kamikazes' dived into the oil tanks at Trincomalee but only one ship, the 'Adamant' was sunk. All the other warships were hidden in the many coves and lagoons of that beautiful part of the island. The few aircraft that were operational went after the enemy; none came back. For unexplained reasons the Japs did not attack Ceylon again.

The result of the brief taste of enemy action was far reaching. Air Commodore d'Albiac and Admiral Leighton arrived to organise the Island's defence. A curfew was ordered and Ceylon's version of the ARP was formed. Cynical residents called it, "The Additional Ration Petrol Corps". The raid created panic among the indigenous population who fled in hordes into the nearest jungle. Running the Naval Hospital without lights, water and domestics tested the ingenuity and stamina of the newly arrived staff. The Sinhalese male nurses and cooks, trained by the nuns before our arrival, were superb and set the good relationship between the races which made our service in Ceylon at that time so happy.

The main railway station in Colombo was an incredible sight after the raid. Masses of terrified Tamils trying to get to India fought to get on the trains. One train slowly moved out. People were hanging like flies on to doors and anything with a finger-hold, swarming over the roofs. Inside the crush was horrifying.

After a week, the Combined Services Authority restored order and the workers came back rather sheepishly and the strange war, in a now mightily prepared Ceylon, changed the lives of everyone living and working there.

I was on my way back to Trincomalee via Colombo after a week's leave in Madras. Flying over Jaffna in the North of Sri Lanka, just as the sun set "with a sizzle" into the sea, the pilot shouted from the flight deck, "The war's over!".

Instead of going to the YWCA, the other eleven passengers whisked me off to the Galle Face Hotel, and we danced the hours away until, at 0530, I had to slip away to catch another Beechcraft to China Bay. I arrived at the airport just in time to see my plane take off. "Don't worry", said the Station Commander, "We'll get you there", and pointed at the only plane on the ground, a tiny Swordfish. (The Swordfish was a two seater by-plane, carried two torpedoes or bombs underneath and was used in attacks on enemy submarines). The 6' 4" Airgunner hoisted me into his cockpit, back to the pilot, climbed on to the fuselage behind me, wrapping his legs around my shoulders, told me to hold on to them. Fifty miles and half an hour later, a clearing the size of a postage stamp appeared in the jungle below. On this we landed to deliver some celebratory liquor to the isolated RAF gun crew. They stared at the sight of me and the Sub-Lieutenant astride the fuselage! Mission completed, we continued, rather erratically, the remaining 50 miles, and somehow I got on duty an unnoticed half an hour late!

Three years ago at a Ceylon lunch in Sussex, a tall, white-haired man asked me what I had been doing in Ceylon. Telling him of my work as a VAD, he said that he had only met one VAD, "a little dark-haired thing - I gave her a lift in my Stringbag (Swordfish) on VJ Day". We had a good laugh together and were so pleased to have met up again.

* * *

VJ Day in Ceylon was, for some reason, very low key. In Trincomalee, Admiral Mountbatten gave a stirring tribute to his Forces from the bridge of one of the battleships anchored off Sober Island, where the rest of the huge Assault Fleet lay waiting to set off to attack and conquer Japan. But the bomb had finished the war and the Fleet, with its thousands of personnel, slipped away to Home bases where the Japanese were too remote to remember.

In December 1945, three months after the Fleet left, my husband, a wartime RNVR Lieutenant, was recalled to his peacetime job as a tea planter. We wanted to have another look at Swamy Rock, a legendary grave of jilted lovers, lured by the goddess to throw themselves over Ceylon's only cliff on to the sea battered rock below. We could not get near the place. Men from the Navy and RAF were pushing hundreds of brand new planes and vehicles over the edge into the swirling sea, jilted and unwanted, like the wretched lovers. A symbolic end to a crazy war. The Jap War was really over.

Staying On

The remains of my January 1942 Ceylon draft had sailed home by the time Dymoke and I left Trincomalee in December 1945 to resume his old job as Manager of Duckwari Group, Rangala.

Nine months before, the Navy had given me "indefinite unpaid sick leave", during which time I worked as a Temporary Woman Assistant in the Dockyard Cypher Office. My work entailed typing decoded signals, and once I was credited with sinking a submarine. The Signals Officer at HQ told everyone that I had made out a signal "HMS Tiptoe" to be scrapped instead of scraped. There were many other flippant accusations, often very rude.

So, my life in the VAD world had been severed, apart from putting up old friends in our waterside bungalow for their "Nights" stand-off.

My two holidays with planters left me with such euphoric feelings of the idyllic life of a planter and I could hardly wait to get to the 2,000 acre Estate and wallow in my new life. We arrived to find the old Dutch bungalow awash after a thunderstorm. One flickering old lamp illuminated our home until a handy husband got the feeble dynamo to work. Kitnan, the old Appu of the previous incumbents, had prepared a meal on the firewood powered stove. The next day six servants in spotless white coats and cloths arrived from the labour force, proficient in their jobs after a crash course with Kitnan. Before long, sinks, handbasins, lavatories and septic tanks had been installed and homely things devised. The image materialised and all was well for fourteen years until the "troubles" forced us to go.

The years of VAD-ing have never been wasted for any of us and one occasion of many comes to mind. My cook, Appu had an inconvenient cold so I concocted a dreadful brew of white mixture (a handy stand-by on C1 at Haslar), crushed aspirin, cinnamon, conchineal and sugar; shook it up and gave the cook a large dose. In three hours he was better. The next morning there was a long queue outside the bungalow. Men, women and children with coughs, colds, sprains, toothache lined up for a dose of "Lady's medicine". This lasted a week when relief came in the form of six month's leave. I referred the ailing hordes to the Estate Apothecary. Not one turned up he told me later.

By staying on I missed the fun of travelling home with the rest of my draft but I found happiness in my chosen life, becoming an authority on what makes a good cup of tea.

SHERBORNE ROYAL NAVAL AUXILIARY HOSPITAL

This is part of the story of Sherborne Royal Naval Auxiliary Hospital.

The prologue was written by Surgeon Lieutenant Commander Charles Langmaid.

Doris Scholefield nee Miller

Beryl Elliott nee Clark

Audrey Beardmore nee Clegg

were all RNVAD who served at Sherborne.

Keith Parkinson JP was an ex-patient.

This is their story of RNH Sherborne.

Mr Charles Langmaid, Surg. Lieut. Commdr. RNVR

Sherborne Royal Naval Auxiliary Hospital was built 1941/1942, probably as an Emergency Medical Service (EMS) hospital but was opened as a Naval establishment early in 1942. I joined the staff in May 1942 at which time there were scarcely any patients there. As a neurosurgeon I was responsible for the treatment of head injuries and peripheral nerve lesions of which there were many. Occasionally there were also true intracranial and spinal lesions. We also had accommodation for orthopaedic, plastic and general surgical cases as well as wards for "medical" conditions. We also had a dentist, a radiologist with a good X-ray department and a pathologist with a well-equipped laboratory. Our patients were sent to us from Haslar RNH Portsmouth and RNH Plymouth because the hospitals on the coast were less safe and, in any case, were kept ready for the admission of acute casualties that might require admission at any time. Our first big test was in August 1942 when there were numerous casualties from the ill-fated, abortive raid on Dieppe, in which mainly Canadian RM personnel were involved. This was regarded as a training exercise for the true invasion which was not to take place for a further two years. We also used to receive patients who had had their primary treatment in the Middle East (Cairo, Tripoli and Tunisia), often in army hospitals or else in hospital ships.

Doris Scholefield nee Miller

The Sherborne Royal Naval Auxiliary Hospital

Doris Scholefield nee Miller

How often we grumbled, or 'dripped' as one said in the Navy, about having to let down hems, get hair cut or dispense with jewellery. I never remember anyone complaining about the hours we worked. On night duty we did a 84 hour week for a month without a night off. We didn't realise then that those years at Sherborne, for many of us, were some of the happiest years of our lives. How sad that it needed a war to give them to us. I had been in a reserved occupation and choose to leave it. I joined the RNVADs in May 1942, was sent to Liverpool for a few months then was drafted to Sherborne where I was very happy. Being called up into the Navy, one expected to be stationed in one of the ports, Portsmouth, Plymouth, Chatham etc. Yet here we were in a beautiful spot. We found ourselves on the top of a hill, above the quaint little Dorset town of Sherborne.

There were forty beds in a ward. Very few patients would be up and about. In surgical wards after an operation most patients were in bed for weeks, not up the day after, as many are in these days.

Admiral's round, when he came to inspect the wards, was a nightmare. At 11 am everything stopped. Saucepans in the galley had to be arranged on shelves in size order like sentinels. No treatments were carried out and no drinks given. Beds had to be in a dead straight line. Worst of all, nobody dare ask for a bedpan. After all this, on one occasion, the Admiral ran his finger along the top of a door and found dust! Oh dear, oh dear!

Four VADs plus a trained QARNNS Sister ran a ward during the day. At night there were only two VADs per ward, plus Sister who covered a number of wards.

To this day, an annual re-union is held in Sherborne. Letters are received from all over the country and the world.

One letter was received from a patient which read:-

> *"I came ashore from an M.T.B.(motor torpedo boat) off Portland in July 1945 and spent some months in Sherborne. My memories of my time there are always happy ones. We were looked after by the most dedicated and attractive girls one could hope to meet. I can remember that when I came into ward F1 that afternoon, I was put between crisp, white sheets and given a boiled egg, cup of tea and toast. Little things they might have been, but they meant so much to me. That was a happy ward, made possible by the nurses who looked after us. On my 21st birthday in August, they produced a birthday cake (in those days of rationing!). I often wonder how they all got on in life. If you can convey to them my appreciation, please do so."*

We had no idea, of course, of the impact these "spoils" had on some of these lads, many of them in their teens.

The hospital consisted of a long colonnade with wards either side leading off. This colonnade was open to the weather. Patients therefore being transported from ward to operating theatre or elsewhere had only a cover over the top of them to protect them from the elements. Having survived having been torpedoed or bombed, what was that inconvenience?

One funny incident on nights. On going on duty I went round the ward to say 'hello' to the patients. Seeing a new face I asked, "What's your problem?". He replied, "Heaps". Puzzled, I went to consult his notes. He had piles!

Sadly the hospital is no more. Following the war it did a wonderful job as a mentally handicapped hospital. It was closed down when it was decided that these places had no further use. It has now been pulled down. So nothing remains but the 'ghosts' of the past.

In 1945, I was sent to Ceylon, unfortunately I got asthma so spent only a few months before being sent back to England on an Aircraft Carrier which was a very interesting trip. I stayed in the RN until 1946.

I would not have missed being an RNVAD for anything. It did us all good, we grew up very quickly and although most young girls of today are more experienced sexually, they did not have our experience of life.

RNH Sherborne

Beryl Christina Elliott nee Clark

I arrived in Sherborne in January 1944. Travelling on the train from Waterloo was another VAD who was returning from leave. She very kindly took me under her wing and on arrival at Sherborne Station she had a taxi waiting to take us to the Royal Naval Auxiliary Hospital. Mr Harold Pitman was the owner and driver of the taxi. While driving up Cheap Street I asked, "Where is the town?". Mr Pitman seemed rather indignant and replied that 'this was it!' I replied that I didn't think I would stay here very long. However, fate decreed otherwise as some months later I was to meet the man who was to become my husband who lived in Sherborne and I am happy to say that I am still here 50 years later.

When we arrived at the VAD Quarters, Margaret, my travelling companion, introduced me to our Commandant, Miss Claire Vian and Miss Margaret Wilkes, the Assistant Commandant, both of whom were addressed as Madam. I was then shown to my cabin which, thankfully, I was to share with my new friend. The cabin consisted of two beds, two built-in wardrobes with a curtain across and one dressing table. There was no door to the cabin, only a green curtain.

Our quarters were shared with the Sisters of QARNNS but they kept to their section and we VADs to ours. We were ruled with a rod of iron by Matron, Miss Campbell. Between her and Miss Vian we had to abide by all the rules and regulations. Miss Vian, who had an Eton crop, horn-rimmed glasses, and most of the time a cigarette hanging from her lips, always wore a navy blue overall. Her bark was much worse than her bite - if one was unwell, she could be very kind. She was so proud of her brother, Admiral Sir Philip Vian of HMS Cossack. Miss Wilkes was a very gentle soul and very kind and, I think, a little afraid of Miss Vian.

Life in a naval shore establishment is run as near as possible to life on board ship - going ashore only when the liberty boat leaves, on the hour and half hour. However, unlike the Wrens and SBAs, we could go "ashore" any time we wished, providing, of course, we were off-duty. We always had to be in by 10 pm unless we had a late pass. When we were granted one, we had to report to Madam's cabin on our return.

Christmas was a riotous time with concerts and parties etc. We really had some very talented staff. The wards were skilfully decorated - the skin ward, for example, was decorated as a ship and called HMS DERMI - an abbreviation of dermatitis.

In retrospect, they were happy days, most of us very young and thrown in at the deep end. There was a wonderful feeling of camaraderie, friendships were made which have lasted unbelievably for 50 years. Margaret, who I met on that January day in 1944, and I are still great friends and meet several times a year. Many of us, staff and ex-patients of RNAH Sherborne are so grateful that we are able to meet each April for our annual reunion. Also, it is remarkable that after so many years we have over 500 members in our VAD (RN) Association. We meet twice a year in London, in June, for our AGM and in November when we go to the Cenotaph.

We all feel so proud that we were privileged to serve in the Royal Navy.

Audrey Beardmore nee Clegg

Arriving Sherborne, Dorset, one dark night in February 1944

Is it really 50 years ago? I remember the night so well, plus three interesting and rewarding years spent at the Royal Naval Hospital Sherborne.

I had a long hard slog of a train journey from Liverpool, no heat, no food, and just one more hazard, I had left my gas mask on Temple Mead station, Bristol, having left the train for five minutes to find a cup of tea. I finally pulled into Yeovil station to be met by rather a snooty Wren driver, who bundled me into the back of a small utility van, whilst she continued her current romance with a Naval Officer.

Audrey is the nurse on the left

It was pitch black when a voice said, "Howdy Ma'am, are you heading for the hospital?". When I recovered from a mini nervous breakdown, I found my unseen companion was an American serviceman, getting a lift to Sherborne. The Wren driver turned out to be very decent, and knowing that the cookhouse would be closed at the hospital, she motored to the WVS Canteen where I got a hot meal after handing in my cap to obtain a knife and fork. Also, she introduced me to a Wren, a Yorkshire girl from near my home town. We became life long friends. She died very suddenly last year, where else but in Sherborne, after she had attended a Wren re-union.

So at last, rather late, I arrived at the Royal Naval Hospital, a series of long brick buildings connected by a lengthy stone colonnade open to the elements.

The only heating in the wards was provided by two coke monstrosities which belched out smoke and dirt. It was mostly an orthopaedic hospital, with two busy theatres and most of the patients were long term. Whilst recuperating they became high spirited, especially after the first shore leave into the town to sample the local cider. Night duty was particularly riotous, where the main object of the up-patients was to play a joke on the unsuspecting night nurse, e.g. tying the night light up with elastic so that when pulled down to keep the ward shady, it shot back to the ceiling. That meant that one had to climb onto the table to fix it, giving a tantalising glimpse of black silk stockinged leg, or perhaps a peep of service issue. What a sight it used to be on concert day in the big hall. I used my bit of talent as a pianist, along with quite a few other talented people, and anybody that could get there, did so. They hobbled, were carried, and even beds trundled down the colonnade. The lads stamped and cheered with Matron and a row of Gold Braid sitting in the plumb seats on the front row.

Sherborne was full of American Servicemen just before D-Day. I got friendly with Scottie, who ran the doughnut dugout, and it was there that I met 'Mert' an Infantry Sergeant. Our rendering of 'Don't Fence Me In' in close harmony often rang out through the streets of Sherborne, as we strolled back to the Hospital. He was due to be shipped to France, and was certain that he would be killed. I wonder if he was.

I could go on reminiscing. Fun in unfunny situations, lots of hard work and long hours, but a lot of laughter. Towards the end, (I've saved the best bit to the end), I met my husband to be, a Royal Marine Commando, wounded crossing the Rhine. He nicknamed Officer's Ward, 'The Sherborne Country Club'. He was there for twelve months, and came and went as he pleased, in between several operations to repair an arm smashed up by a sniper's bullet. Finally after being demobbed in 1946, we married, his version being that he must have proposed whilst under the anaesthetic. Not true. We always intended to make our home in the lovely county of Dorset, but it wasn't to be. So we are now content with our yearly visit to the Hospital re-union, held each year in April. We both have very fond memories of Sherborne, and trust that there will be many more visits to come.

Keith Parkinson JP

There was only one place to lie if you were seriously wounded as a result of D-Day - RNH Sherborne. I was sent to RNH Sherborne after my craft, HM Landing Craft Flak 1 was sunk by human torpedo on 17th August 1944 at 0555 hrs. The ex-Cross Channel Steamer (now a Hospital Ship) brought me back to Portsmouth and RNH Haslar (first operations on the second-hand Hospital Ship, second operations at RNH Haslar) but I was now slipping away fast, so they sent me to RNH Sherborne for amputation of my right leg, gangrene had set in, but joining the Royal Marines as a boy and just being 18 years old they could only amputate with my fathers permission. So "Telegram to Dad", who replied, "Mend it, he's a regular RM".

In weeks and months that followed, I saw such devotion by RN Surgeons and VADs at RNH Sherborne which would fill a book on its own. The Matron, with her stare, could stop blood flowing. Sister Strickland was so beautiful, she outshone Betty Grable and you forgot anyone you had left back home.

A long time later it was VE Day and Matron said, "Everyone to be in by 10 pm", so I volunteered to open the French windows at midnight for the nurses. Yes, I was caught by Matron. Next morning I was ushered into the Rear Admiral's (Surgeon) room and sent to Lewiston Manor as punishment six months sooner than I should have been. Our course of rehabilitation was riding second hand bikes; if you had lost a right leg, the right-hand peddle was removed and vice versa. I recall stacking hay and corn in surrounding fields, and putting out the house fire caused by the thatched roof catching fire. Rumour had it that Lewiston Manor belonged to the Rose's Lime Juice people. There was a beautiful music room always locked against RM & RN personnel.

There are so many wonderful memories of the people of Sherborne, they worked so hard to improve life for all the wounded, for instance, if they knew you smoked they would leave whatever 'cigs' were left in their packets on your lap, always brought you a drink, invited you to their homes. Pub landlords were the kindest and friendliest I've ever met.

In conclusion, may I say, "Thank God we had RNH Sherborne, its staff and most of all good, sound Dorset people, salt of the earth". I still have two good legs thanks to Lt Comm. O'Brien.

Eileen Thom

Eileen sadly died in August 1993 but kind permission has been given by her sister, for her memoirs to be published. She was always happy-go-lucky and well-liked by everyone.

Joyce Drury

Crail to Colombo

Crail in Fife was the home of HMS Jackdaw, a Fleet Air Arm station and I, with four other VADs, worked in the Sick Quarters in the town with two Naval Sisters and Wrens.

Eileen Thom

The signal recalling me to Kingseat, Aberdeenshire, for posting to Colombo, was the most exciting thing and off I went North in the train. (The nearest railway now is 14 miles away). Kingseat was the base for most RNVADs in Scotland. It was a requisitioned mental home about 18 miles from Aberdeen. Here it was we learnt the language of the Navy, 'deck', 'cabin', 'going ashore', etc. and the discipline.

When I was first called up to Kingseat in 1941, we had our worst weather for years, with snow two feet deep and huge drifts. Patients were brought up in horse drawn sledges and the cold in the nurses' home was intense. I was given home leave for Christmas but had no means of getting to St Andrews, some ninety miles away. However, one of the Wrens and an SBA and I decided to walk to Dyce where we thought we would get a train. It was six miles hard slog in the snow. The SBA gave up but we got there and the incredulous Station Master heaped coal on the fire and made us tea and toast with precious raspberry jam.

Also posted to Ceylon was Winnie Young and a third VAD. While waiting for our medicals we were looked after by a nice, fair haired girl. I sat with my legs up on the mantelpiece draining my varicose veins! Winnie and I passed but the third girl failed her medical. The fair haired nurse looking after us told us she was coming too, Kate Henry!

Miss Cook, our Commandant, and Miss Glass saw us off at the station and we were on our way to Liverpool to meet up with thirty Haslar girls. Our overnight carriage was shared with three RAF pilots, home from the Azores laden with bottles of gin, whisky and brandy which they insisted on sharing with us. They seemed determined to float us down to Liverpool. Once there my diary records that the Haslar girls seemed a glamorous lot but did not seem particularly friendly. Little did we know that some would become lifelong friends. We finally boarded 'La Reina Del Pacifico' and, to our amazement, we three were ushered into a first class cabin with four bunks, the fourth being taken by Jane Scarth. Someone was heard to remark darkly that the Purser must have been a Scot!

In the July 1986 newsletter, Beryl Salter gave a graphic description of the bombing our convoy underwent in the Mediterranean. My diary records that we three sat on Katie's lower bunk holding hands and thinking of the girls in the dormitories so far below and so crowded. Reaching Bombay, one of my most vivid memories was standing with Nancy McCormack watching the troops leaving the ship. It was still dark and the decks were floodlit. We were both weeping but the troops were laughing and cheerful. (Does anyone know what happened to the delightful Nancy?).

After four days in Bombay we started our train journey to Ceylon, stopping at Madras for Christmas Day. Some of us stayed with Sir Hugh and Lady Hood where we had baths in hot, fresh water and our dresses were washed and ironed for us before boarding the train again for Ceylon. The beautiful island of Ceylon, the lushness, the birds, the hospital in Colombo, the dengue fever that hit all of us new girls and, finally, the room in Sisters' Quarters with Dorothy Jacobs, as she was then, just engaged to her Mr Lewes.

It is all so long ago, a lifetime ago, but the bonding remains and it is with such pleasure that we meet up with our friends from those far off days. We are all elderly now but on meeting the years roll away and we can see again the girls with whom we laughed and worked.

Beryl M. Salter nee Harris

Sadly, Beryl died in April 1993 but her husband has given kind permission to use her story. Beryl's ashes were committed to sea three miles off the mouth of the Tyne by HMS Orwell in August 1993.

Joyce Drury

Beryl and Laurrie Salter

I joined St John Ambulance in 1933 as a cadet. In 1938 I enrolled in the civil nursing reserve, did my training at Bournemouth and Boscombe. Whilst at Boscombe hospital we nursed the survivors from the Dieppe raid. At the outbreak of war I volunteered as a RNVAD. Subsequently I was called for service in the Royal Navy and served at Haslar then Minton Magna RN hospitals, before going to RNAH Colombo. I didn't know my future husband was on an escort ship with the convoy which was picking up survivors from the sunken vessels.

Journey to Ceylon, November/December 1943

On a cold November morning about thirty of us trudged through Liverpool docks looking for the ship on which we were to sail to the Far East. Miss Waistell, our Commandant, had told us that the number was G10R (Ceylon), so we

Going on night duty during an air raid.
The night's food supply in the basket
Gas masks always carried.

Drawing by Marcelle Dawson nee Grennan

called out to the men lining the rails of each ship we passed, until we identified ours, we embarked to wolf whistles from thousands of Commandos, who were going out to join 'Operation Zipper'.

We sailed the next day, with only the dockers to wave us 'good-bye'. We realised we were in convoy when we heard the escorts instructing the ships to zigzag . . . one 'whoop' for port, two 'whoops' for starboard.

The journey through the Atlantic was uneventful, though some RN chiefs who could read the Aldis lamp signals told us that there were U-boats in the area. We sailed west almost to America, and then south past the Canary Islands. Ten days later we saw the lights of Morocco to our starboard. That evening we sailed through the Straits of Gibraltar, the Rock, with a faint light atop, seen in silhouette.

The next afternoon, immediately astern of our ship, up popped what we thought was a U-boat, and we were relieved to see a British sailor walk aft and run up the White Ensign! Up to this time we had had no cover at all. A little later, when an aircraft flew round the convoy, we waved madly, thinking it was the RAF at last! But this was no RAF plane, and shortly the klaxons sounded and we had to go below, while wave after wave of Stuka dive bombers attacked the convoy.

Beryl Salter *right,* **Peggy Hamal** *left,* **at Minton Magna**

We sat in our cabins, greatcoats on, passports and Red Cross cards in our pockets, 'Blondie' (Kay Clarke) entertained us with her tap dancing. Peggy Greathead said nothing would stop her afternoon bath, and Judy Lewthwaite played 'Transatlantic Lullaby' on her portable gramophone. All this time the ship was shuddering as the bombs exploded around her. We had to go down three more decks to supper when the bugle went at 18.30 - nothing would interfere with the ship's routine! Below the water line the shuddering was more pronounced! The Stukas' bombing raid stopped at about 20.00 hours. When we went up to the boat deck to get some air, it reeked of hot Oerlikons which had been fired for nearly five hours.

The next morning the RN Captain i/c (in command) Naval draft drew particular attention to the red lights on our life-jackets, remarking that they had saved many lives after the Stuka raid the previous evening. These intensive bombing raids continued for several days, the Stukas coming in out of the sun each evening. It was strictly forbidden to open the portholes during these raids, but we did so, and watched the destroyers and cruisers of the escort tearing up and down among the convoy with their guns blazing. As we travelled further east out of range of the Stukas, our escorts had to contend with German E-boats.

We reached Aden safely. The harbour was crammed with merchant ships, many with great holes in their sides. We stayed at Aden for five days but were not allowed ashore, as we had the Commandos on board. However, the RAF stationed in Aden came aboard, and we enjoyed their concert immensely.

The convoy was re-formed, and was then escorted by ships of the Royal Indian Navy, including an aircraft-carrier which provided planes for anti-submarine patrols. The observer on one plane signalled our ship 'Who is the girl in the yellow pyjamas?' (Maxine Housden). One pilot missed the deck and landed 'in the drink'. A loud-hailer announced that he had been saved, but the plane was lost.

On arrival at Bombay some five days later we rushed to the nearest post office to send off cables home. (People at home had heard over the wireless that a convoy had been bombed, with the loss of some ships, and that there were Naval nurses travelling in the convoy). A few days later we travelled by train to Madras, where we arrived on Christmas Day and were entertained by some British families before leaving that night for the sea crossing to Ceylon.

I met Laurrie when he was a hospital patient in Colombo suffering with dysentery. I was attracted to him right away, it was not long before he proposed and asked me to marry him. Logic took over, I realised I knew nothing about him. Laurrie suggested I asked Chris Chambers (another VAD) who knew his family and was his best friend's sister. She said that it was a lovely family. Then a year later he was being drafted back to sea from his position with the C in C staff as assistant Admiralty overseer ashore. We decided to marry on his embarkation leave and spent our honeymoon in the jungle in a 15 cwt truck staying with the Veddas who are aboriginal pigmy people. On the way back to Columbo the truck broke down. Laurrie left me with the village headman while he and a boy made the 16 miles to the next village for oil. When he returned I was surrounded by all the village women who had brought their babies for me to see and brought gifts of coconuts, pineapples and many fruits. It was a honeymoon to remember.

After VJ day, Laurie was drafted to Bombay. This was during the Partition troubles in India. He came down to Columbo to escort me. On reaching Madras, he was made O/C (officer in charge) Train to evacuate service woman from Madras to Bombay. The town was in chaos due to the rioting and we had to be there a few days before we could reach the railway station. When we left Madras the journey to Bombay took five days during which we went through the junction about which John Masters wrote his book 'Bhawanha Junction'. We were shunted in and out of the station all day. On arrival, Bombay Victoria station was on fire. The Army was in full force with trucks to collect the women and children. On return to England we lived in Staffordshire for a while then moved to Newcastle on Tyne.

Beryl Salter and honeymoon truck, Taken in Columbo, January 1945.

Beryl continued with her St John Ambulance Brigade work and became County Officer to nursing cadets and was eventually awarded the Order of St John.

Taken in Columbo, January 1945.

Drawing by Marcelle Dawson nee Grennan

Maude Norman

Maude Norman has written a book, which she has been unable to get published. I have agreed to publish extracts along with the memoirs of other VADs. It is sad that so many good books cannot get into print.

Joyce Drury

Taken at RNAH Diyatalawa 1944,
Front left to right: **Patient, Nurse Morrison, Maude Norman, Patient.**

"We're carrying meat", said an officer who surveyed us at the foot of the gangway. "It's a good cargo to have in these times. If a ship gets holed or develops a list, carcasses don't shift like grain, and they don't explode".

* * *

Dusk was falling on a September evening, 1942, as a party of volunteers from countries in South America was assembled on the quayside in Buenos Aires and divided into two groups; one to board the handsome liner Andalucia Star, and the other the more modest Esperance Bay. I was in the second group.

Good-byes had all been said. Ships moving in and out of neutral ports were spared unwelcome attention, and there was no gathering of well-wishers to see us off. Talk was subdued as anxious eyes were turned to the ships, their outlines illusive against the brown water and the darkening sky. Some who had hoped to travel together found they would not be doing so, and as the groups moved apart there were a few exchanges of 'Good Luck', 'Safe Crossing', or 'See you in London', with voices lowered as though afraid of tempting Fate. The Andalucia Star was the first to raise her gangway and cast off, and those of us left stood waving silently as she moved out into the river.

The normal sea routes linking the Pacific coast of South America with Europe had been abandoned with the closure of the Panama Canal, and at this time merchant shipping was operating only from Atlantic ports. Passages were hard to come by and were not to be risked. Our contingent from Chile had crossed the continent by rail a fortnight earlier as a precaution against the Andean pass at Uspallata being blocked by snow, which frequently happens in winter and early spring. In places the line had just been cleared and, at a height of some 12,500 feet, our train crawled between glittering walls stacked carriage high, while workmen, muffled and gloved, paused in their shovelling to cheer us on our way. Down at Mendoza we changed trains to traverse the vast fertile plains of Argentina. Much of the food produced on those rich farmlands was destined for countries overseas. The hazards of transporting it had never been so great.

* * *

The first night we crossed the River Plate (Rio de La Plata), and in the morning took on more meat for Britain at Montevideo, the Uruguayan capital. Though the country was officially neutral, the people of Uruguay were for the most part pro-Ally, and on the dockside we were greeted warmly and showered with good wishes. These were also directed at another party of volunteers who came aboard just before we sailed.

On our way out of the river we skirted the partly submerged wreck of the German pocket battleship Graf Spee, lying where she had been scuttled at the time of the Battle of the River Plate, while the Royal Navy cruisers Exeter and Ajax and the Royal New Zealand Navy cruiser Archilles waited for her outside territorial waters. It was in December 1939 that the three cruisers came upon and engaged their formidable adversary in the river estuary. Though heavily outgunned in their combined force, they inflicted on her - but also suffered - considerable damage, and the Graf Spee put in to Montevideo for urgent repairs. Just before the expiry of her time limit in a neutral port, the Nazi High Command ordered that, rather than return to the engagement, the battleship should be sunk forthwith. Accordingly she was taken out of the port and consigned to her shallow and inglorious grave. Three days later her captain committed suicide in Buenos Aires.

I remember the ferment of excitement in Santiago over these happenings. Chile has strong traditional ties of friendship with the Royal Navy. In particular HMS Exeter and Ajax held a warm place in the hearts of the Chilean people, whose concern for the outcome of that battle being fought on the other side of the continent, and for the fate of the British seamen, stemmed from an event much nearer home. Having sailed away after completing a courtesy visit to Chilean stations in January 1939, these ships had returned to the port of Talcahuano on learning that a devastating earthquake had struck the south of the country. Ashore their men had provided immediate and precious help in rescue operations, and later they had taken aboard many people whose homes had been destroyed, transferring them to places further north which had escaped serious damage. As friends in time of trouble, and as ambassadors of goodwill, they are not forgotten.

But there was too an element of sadness, and of sympathy for a gallant Naval officer forced to carry out an order which went counter to all his traditions. While in Buenos Aires arranging for the burial of his dead and the care of his wounded before ending his life, Captain Lansdorf was reported to have spoken highly of the skill and the bravery of his wartime enemies.

* * *

Aboard ship one lost the sense of constant danger - or very nearly - and settled into the wartime routine. The Esperance Bay and her crew were seasoned veterans in the battle for survival.

Ship's captains exercised their discretion in demanding emergency procedures. On our ship passengers were allocated muster stations but not a particular boat, which, in the event of an attack, might be rendered useless. In cases of need we would be directed to the available boats or rafts. The lifeboats, with their precious drinking water, were inspected and swung out on their davits every day. Blackout regulations were strict and were observed scrupulously. Smoking on deck after dark was forbidden, and at no time must there be shouting, singing, or the playing of musical instruments in the open. Male passengers took turns at lookout duty and were given elementary training in the manning of the ship's guns. Everyone watched the sea by day, when every speck - real or imagined - suggested a possible periscope. We zigzagged continually, so that our wake described a jagged and ever-changing pattern, and the direction of the sun varied from one minute to another.

We were, of course, provided with life-jackets, so called. These consisted of two hard - presumably buoyant- rectangular cushions, attached to a harness, to be worn back and front of the chest like sandwich boards. Some people protested that these were an obsolete type, and certainly they were very different from the jackets worn by the crew. Whatever their merits or otherwise, from these contraptions we were never parted day or night. In addition we were advised to carry with us at all times our lifeboat survival bags, containing protective clothing against cold or tropical sun, simple first-aid necessities, and specified iron rations, which included a tin of sweetened condensed milk, with a nail firmly attached. There were times on that voyage when it became a great temptation to broach some of the contents, particularly the small bottle of brandy labelled 'For medicinal use only'. Personal papers, in water-tight packs, were worn on a belt, and at times we were advised to sleep fully clothed.

Our route or position were not spoken of. The South Atlantic was cold and grey but as the sun gained in strength, and flying fishes and porpoises made their appearance, we imagined seeing besides these enchanting creatures, other more sinister shapes lurking under the surface. Enemy U-boats were reported to be particularly active around the western bulge of Africa and in the vicinity of the Canary Islands and the Azores.

We had seen no craft of any kind since leaving the River Plate, when one morning somebody playing deck quoits remarked that we were no longer zigzagging, and it was evident that we were gathering speed. Quickly the word went round that we were being pursued by an unidentified ship, and clearly she was gaining on us. Excitement was tense as a menacing shape appeared on the horizon and the distance shortened. A report rang out. Our spurt of speed was halted and in a surprisingly short distance we came to a stop. Was this friend or foe? Were we to be captured - or sunk? And would the Esperance Bay offer resistance? Encouraged by the fact that we were not ordered off the deck, fear gave way to fascination as, pressed against the rails, we watched our pursuer draw alongside and lower a boat. All was well. It was a destroyer of the United States Navy that had challenged the Esperance Bay and when apparently not entirely satisfied as to her identity, had ordered the ship to stop and was sending a boarding party to investigate. We were able to talk to some of the Americans. They told us that the area they were patrolling was 'lousy with German U-boats' and that many Allied ships were being sunk in those waters. They could escort us only for a little way. They hoped we would make port safely. So did we!

We reached Freetown, Sierra Leone, the following afternoon. The boom - a huge submarine-proof net - was drawn aside by tugs to let us in, and immediately closed behind us. The harbour was full of Allied shipping. As we approached our allotted berth, we were surprised to hear cries of 'Viva Chile!' and some of us to be hailed by name. We were passing alongside a Free French liner, the President Doumergue, and on her decks, waving and cheering, we made out some of the volunteers from Chile who had left Buenos Aires the same night as ourselves, aboard the Andalucia Star. The next day a few of them managed to come across to the Esperance Bay and told us their story. The Andalucia Star, travelling alone, had been torpedoed a few nights earlier, when a humane submarine commander had allowed time for everyone to get off the ship before she was finally sunk with a third torpedo. After spending two nights in lifeboats, they were picked up by a Royal Navy corvette, and taken into Freetown Harbour. They were none the worse for their ordeal, and in good spirits, but of course had lost all their belongings, and we gave them what we could in the way of clothing, cosmetics etc. They were expecting to be taken off the President Doumergue and to continue their journey on another British ship very shortly. We knew that the Andalucia Star was the last remaining ship of the old-established Blue Star Line operating on that route. German U-boats had accounted for them all, and for the lives of many of their passengers.

We remained in Freetown Harbour for just over a week, but were not allowed ashore. During our stay the Esperance Bay took aboard a party of convalescent RAF personnel on their way from Bathurst, Gambia. In those men we saw for the first time some of the ravages caused by tropical diseases. Most of them were exhausted by repeated attacks of malaria; all were yellow-skinned, either from jaundice or from prophylactic drugs. None had the energy or enthusiasm for shipboard activities. They took a poor view of travelling by sea in wartime 'like sitting ducks'; they would feel much safer in the air.

We were all impatient to be on our way. From the boat deck we would watch planes of the Vichy French forces stationed in Dakar, flying round the perimeter of the harbour, and no doubt keeping the Germans informed of the movement of Allied ships. We saw no Allied planes at any stage of our journey.

When we left the harbour at last, it was under cover of darkness. In the morning we found we were travelling with a convoy. It consisted of ships of all sizes, ages and speeds, each no doubt carrying a vitally important cargo. We never knew the actual number that set out; we could rarely see any but the ships immediately around us, and even these disappeared from view at times when visibility was bad, and we seemed to be alone on the ocean. The shortage of escort vessels at the time was acute, and that large, unwieldy flotilla was said to be escorted only by two destroyers and three corvettes. At times one of the latter could be seen doubling back to round up stragglers, while we all slowed down to wait for them.

A few nights out, a brilliantly illuminated vessel, travelling under the flag of a neutral state, cut right across our convoy, shedding her light on a number of the blacked-out ships. There seemed to be something sinister in this encounter, but perhaps it was only coincidence.

The following night we had just sat down to dinner when there was a resounding crash! It was as if a crane-load of bricks or concrete slabs had been dropped from a great height on to the deck above. No one moved until the alarm was sounded and the order given, and no one spoke, but in those seconds as we looked at each other across the tables, I saw that every face went dead white - as no doubt mine did too. There followed another thunderous but more distant bang as, in silent and orderly fashion, we filed out and climbed seemingly endless flights of stairs, struggling to get into the harness and fasten the straps of our despised life-jackets. Most of us had - alas - left our lifeboat bags in our cabins; too late now to go back for them!

On the boat deck we were mustered behind overlapping blackout screens, and so were spared the sight of the ship on our starboard breaking up and sinking. We knew her to be the French liner President Doumergue; we were uncertain whether the survivors from the Andalucia Star had been taken off her in Freetown Harbour, and we were not assured of their safety until we arrived in London.

Everyone knew and accepted that a convoy must keep going, and that it was only the escort vessels that might stop and search for survivors, but a sense of impotent guilt persisted with the thought that people - perhaps ones friends - might be struggling in the water or hanging on to overcrowded boats, while other ships went on regardless. An officer who had seen it all told us that this was a case where nobody could possibly have been saved and he snapped his fingers as he described how, following one mighty blast, the French ship had simply disintegrated and gone under. Perhaps she was carrying explosives.

There was nothing to be said in the face of such finality. One anxiety that no one spoke of at the time, but that I heard later was in many minds, was the fact that our antiquated 'life-jackets' had no lights. When telling us about the sinking of the Andalucia Star and the rescue operations, our friends had described how a number of survivors, unable to get into the boats, and drifting on the surface, had been located only by the lights they carried.

The hours passed slowly as we stood packed together behind the screens, braced for another explosion. None came, and about midnight we were allowed to return to our cabins, suddenly aware that we were very hungry as well as frightened.

In the morning we found ourselves in the middle of the front line of the convoy. It was said that the Commodore ship had been the victim of that second explosion the previous night, and that we had moved into her place. It was a sultry, windless day; the sky was leaden; the sea lay smooth as silk - pregnant with menace. Two ships within sight were re-fuelling from tankers. Our progress was painfully slow. No one doubted that enemy U-boats were travelling with us. Indeed, during the afternoon one surfaced briefly right under the stern of Esperance Bay - too close for the rear gun to be trained on her. We received a graphic account of this happening from one of the stewards who was also a member of the the gun crew, and whose anger and frustration we shared. The ship carried depth charges, but it was said that their use at slow speed in a convoy could be suicidal.

That night dinner was put forward by half an hour and, though reluctant to go below, we hoped to get some. But it was not to be. Before any food made its appearance, there came an unmistakable crash. We froze in our seats waiting for the order to move, delayed, no doubt while more important matters were dealt with. By the time we reached the top deck there could be felt a mighty vibration, as the Esperance Bay put on her top speed and tore away from the convoy. Our cargo was precious. Our relief was enormous; to be free of that slow-moving target. Later I was appalled to learn from friends in the Admiralty that the convoy had lost fourteen ships. We had felt impatient at the slowness of some of the small and ancient vessels that held us back, yet their cargoes were just as vital to Britain's war effort as ours, and they were much more vulnerable.

Our wireless officer intercepted a claim by the Germans that they had sunk the Esperance Bay - an understandable mistake, since we had left a gap in the convoy. Whilst appreciating the joke, some of us feared that this claim would be broadcast in their news and propaganda bulletins to Latin America - as indeed it was, causing needless anxiety in a number of homes.

We knew nothing of our whereabouts as we journeyed on, moving a good deal faster on our own. The intense cold and the heavy seas that buffeted the ship for some days suggested that we had gone into far northern waters. It was surmised that we were passing round the north of Ireland, and would approach by the North Channel, but of course we never knew. One night the lookouts reported a ship on fire on the horizon, and we were warned that there might be trouble ahead, but there were no further incidents, and gradually the weather improved.

We had been at sea for six weeks when we were told to be ready to disembark early the following morning; we were approaching the British Isles. Then for two interminable and frustrating days, all shipping lay paralysed by fog in the Mersey, thankful for an umbrella of sausage-like barrage balloons.

When, at long last, we stepped ashore at Liverpool, our first thought was to send off reassuring messages to our homes. The ordeal of the Atlantic was over for us; not so for the men who would turn the ship about and go back again and again into the troubled seas.

The Esperance Bay, a vessel of the Australian Shaw-Saville Line, survived the war, as I was delighted to learn when she berthed in Singapore Harbour in 1946.

Note: Volunteers from Argentina, Chile, Peru, Uruguay, and the Falkland Islands made this trip on the Esperance Bay. The many volunteers from Brazil and countries in the north of the continent took ships sailing from ports further up the Atlantic coast.

* * *

The purpose of the journey was, of course, to join HM Forces. Young people of British descent had been making their way to the United Kingdom since the outbreak of war, as in many cases their fathers or other relatives had done during World War I. Some of the volunteers had spent their school days in Britain, later returning to join their families and to take up employment in South America, while others knew Britain only at second hand, and were moved by family tradition and ties of sentiment.

Volunteer's Committees in the different countries provided help and advice. They assisted in obtaining release from employment and secured passages on such ships as were available.

However, not everyone could get away at once. My difficulties were considerable. I had signed up as a volunteer in the first week of the war, but was told by my employers - Shell-Mex Chile - that I could not be released. As secretary, my post was confirmed by Shell Headquarters in London as a 'reserved occupation'. I was asked to work at the British Embassy in Santiago, who would, if necessary, 'requisition' my services from Shell. Allied war propaganda abroad had assumed great importance. I was to act as PA to a newly appointed and immensely dynamic Press Attaché. Material supplied to the local press had to be edited in accordance with a daily guidance cable from the Ministry, indicating what items of war news were to be highlighted and which played down, and each evening I scanned quantities of material submitted by our correspondents, blue-pencilling accordingly.

Apart from my duties at the Press Office, I filled another less obvious post. After being interviewed at the Chancellery, I had been asked to report to a man who occupied a small, separate office, within the Embassy grounds. He greeted me with a quizzical smile as, briefly and graphically, he made plain his role, and asked me if I would be prepared to work with 'us'. I stopped him short to ask whether he knew that I was not a British subject. "Indeed yes", he said. "We have a complete dossier on you". (I still sometimes wonder who could have investigated me). The demands of this aspect of my job were spasmodic. From time to time I would be presented to a stranger, whom I was unlikely to meet again. I understood little, and was content not to know too much about reports which I took down and transcribed, and of which I retained no copies. On leaving such sessions, or when carrying material, I was instructed to travel by taxi. I was told that my eventual release would be dependent on finding a suitable replacement. The Ambassador, Sir Charles Orde, was sympathetic, and he meantime pulled strings on my behalf, so that finally the Foreign Office authorised my acceptance as a volunteer for war service in the United Kingdom. By mid 1942 the Press Office in Santiago was well staffed and a member of the Ambassador's family took on the 'confidential role'.

* * *

In the early part of the war there had been doubts as to whether volunteers from abroad were really wanted by Britain. By 1942 no such doubts remained; they were. Recruiting officers from the different services boarded the Esperance Bay on arrival, and some people who had already made their choice signed on and received instructions there and then. However, we had been assured that there was no need to make an immediate decision. I was anxious, if at all possible, to do work with medical connections, though I realised that my choice might be limited by my nationality.

* * *

The River Plate London Committee, with Headquarters in River Plate House, Finsbury Circus, took good care of the thousands of men and about eight hundred women volunteers from Latin America. The Committee kept in touch with us wherever we were posted and received and forwarded our mail.

* * *

On our arrival at Euston Station, some of our party were met and taken off by relatives or friends who could put them up. The rest of us were escorted to the Royal Veterinary College in Camden Town, a part of which had been converted to provide temporary accommodation for homeless arrivals from overseas.

Though she had never met me before, Moira Hale came to my rescue on hearing that I had landed with a severely sprained ankle and she invited me to stay at her home until I could make other arrangements. Many of us who arrived as strangers remember gratefully the hospitality we received at Moira's wonderfully elastic flat in Sloane Avenue. Her spare room was always available to me for week-end leave, and we became lasting friends.

* * *

Exploring, sight-seeing and visiting, we made the most of our remaining freedom. There was an undeniable magic in the spirit of wartime London. The blackout came as no surprise and - apart from the risk of enemy action - those dark streets were much safer than we are ever likely to know them again with all the lights on. I was tremendously impressed by the system of food rationing, and also relieved that shortages were not even more severe. One felt assured that, whatever the cost in lives and ships, vital supplies would continue to be maintained.

* * *

Before being accepted in a service hospital, VADs had to complete a brief period of practical training in a civilian hospital. To this end I was first directed to Middlesex Hospital, W1, where I presented myself carrying a letter of introduction from the Commandant of my detachment. A super-starchy looking woman, whom I understood to be the Assistant Matron, glanced briefly at the letter, and declared that Middlesex Hospital did not accept aliens. No regrets were expressed. This was the first, and indeed the only time that I was made to feel an unwelcome outsider.

However, the following day I was received kindly by University College Hospital in Gower Street, where I was helped and given every opportunity to see and to learn as much as possible in the time available, and I was there when I received my summons to RN Hospital Haslar.

The Navy! I was overjoyed! At interview I had been unable to claim family links with any of the services and was told that I should probably be called for the Army, but with my roots in a maritime country with a fine seafaring tradition, it was natural that I should feel drawn to the Navy. Later I was to learn just how lucky I was, because only the Senior Service extended to its nurses the privileges of first class travel, access to officers' clubs and shops etc. - all of which made a great difference in the next few years, especially overseas.

* * *

Miss Waistell, the VAD Commandant, interviewed each new arrival individually. As I waited my turn on a draughty staircase on a cold December morning, I couldn't help wondering how this formidable lady felt about aliens. But my fears were soon allayed. The wise old eyes that looked into mine were unmistakably friendly. Indicating the papers before her, she boomed her welcome, "Well, Norman, you have come a long way to help us, how splendid!"

Naval jargon was bewildering at first, but one soon picked it up. We quickly learned to refer to the floor as the deck, and the wall as the bulkhead. Rooms became cabins, and the kitchen was always the galley, while - strangest of all - the lavatory was known as the heads. This term was new to me when I first received instructions about a patient who was to be 'allowed up to heads only' - a puzzling message for the uninitiated!

Naval shore establishments were styled 'ships', and enjoyed the feminine gender. Leaving their premises was known as 'going ashore' and authorised absence was 'shore leave', while absence without leave, or late return, was being 'adrift' - a situation not to be recommended!

Once, after an action in the Channel, the casualties included a surprising and endearing patient. Cradled protectively in the arms of a stretcher case, and comforted with soothing talk, came Debbie, the ship's cat, suffering from a crushed forepaw. Duly registered as a member of the ship's company injured in action, her paw was X-rayed and splinted under a light anaesthetic, and pussy was nursed with as much devotion as any seaman. Moreover, she was allowed to share a bed with one or another of them! In true Nelsonian tradition, Authority turned a blind eye.

* * *

In the early part of 1943, Britain's alliance with Soviet Russia was being fostered in the forefront of international diplomacy. On Sunday, February 21st, a pageant was held in the Albert Hall in London to celebrate Red Army Day and Russia's impressive victories over her recent ally - Nazi Germany. The whole affair was shrouded in secrecy beforehand, and indeed few people not immediately concerned knew about it; but it must have been considered important judging by the very distinguished persons who took part, and it was fully reported in the press after the event. (I was later assured that a film was made of this pageant, and it was shown on television a few years ago). All the fighting forces were represented, and also key civilian services; munitions workers, farmers, fishermen, firemen, police, etc. Nurses from the principal service hospitals took part, and I was one of six VADs representing Haslar.

We went up to London three days before the affair, under the wing of the Assistant Commandant, and stayed at the VAD Ladies' Club - then in Cavendish Square. Most of our time was spent rehearsing at the Hall, under the direction of an RN Commander, who showed commendable patience with our ineptitude. VADs were not trained to march, and in order to reach the arena we had to negotiate a very awkward little flight of steps. Again and again we practised our entry; left foot over the first step, and then a frantic effort to 'keep up' without treading on the heels of the person in front. To make matters worse, we followed immediately behind the WRNS, whose performance was superb. However, if our marching was far from perfect, our crisp white caps were feminine, the big red crosses on our aprons made a fine splash of colour among the more sombre uniforms, and, as nurses, we received a tremendous ovation.

It was good to get away from service life at times. When off duty I was assured of a welcome at the home of two charming and individualistic elderly ladies to whom I had been introduced by their old friend, Miss Waistell. Like her, the Misses Dorrien-Smith belonged to a family noted for services to their country, and both had been VADs during World War I. Their interests and activities were very wide, and at their lovely old-world cottage by the sea I met some delightful people. While prevented by wartime restrictions from sailing their yacht, they had busied themselves by making some exquisite models, and they were confident of resuming their favourite hobby as soon as the war was over. They had both travelled widely - not always to the same parts of the world - and one sister had visited South America on two occasions. Poring nostalgically over her diaries, we were delighted to find entries about people and places of mutual interest, and her sketches included some very familiar Chilean scenes.

* * *

From time to time, a notice would appear in the VAD mess calling for volunteers for service overseas. The destination of the intended draft was not mentioned. It was largely a matter of who saw the notice before the list was closed, because there were many who hoped to see something of the world.

I managed to get my name on a list that spring of 1943, though I doubted whether I had served long enough to be eligible.

* * *

Early in the summer of 1943, I was included in a small draft to Worthy Down, near Winchester, where new sick quarters were to be opened to serve a Fleet Air Arm training establishment. This was said to be an indefinite posting, and it promised to be interesting.

At the station, we were welcomed by a Surgeon-Commander RN, who helped us to load our luggage into a small van before driving us to our destination. Having noticed an old label on one of my cases, he asked me where I came from, and went on to talk of the hospitality he had received when his ship visited the Chilean naval bases at Valparaiso and Talcahuano.

That summer of 1943 was one to remember, and the fine weather held throughout my fortnight of annual leave, which I spent in Scotland. There I was made welcome by a friend who had been a colleague in Shell-Mex Chile, Santiago, and who was living in Gullane with a small son, while her husband, serving in the RNVR, was on a minesweeper 'somewhere'. We had, of course, much news to exchange. The countryside was beautiful, and the incredibly long hours of daylight were beguiling. As the days flew, I was torn between swimming in the Firth of Forth, and exploring the lovely city of Edinburgh, home of my maternal ancestors. Strolling in Princes Street I was impressed by the number of Poles in Air Force uniform, and I also came across many Canadians. I studied the 1914-1918 War Memorials, and saw that the VADs had been given a prominent place among the women's services.

Back at Winchester I barely had time to settle into my corner of our attic and get to know new staff and new patients when I was recalled to Haslar for foreign draft.

* * *

Excitement was at fever heat! A foreign draft was imminent! Naval VADs recalled from all parts of the country were pouring into Haslar. Speculation and rumours were rife.

"Hullo! You on this draft? Oh, good!"
"Know where we're going? There seem to be a lot of us!"
"Jane thinks it's somewhere in India."
"Well, I expect we'll soon hear."

And we hadn't long to wait. That evening, Madam called us together and told us that we would shortly be leaving for a place called Diyatalawa, in Ceylon, where we were required for the opening of a new RN auxiliary hospital in the hill country. The climate was said to be good.

We were to proceed on embarkation leave the following day. We must get full tropical kit as quickly as possible. It was also suggested that we should be prepared for quite a good social life, including sporting activities.

On return from leave we would remain at Haslar until we sailed. Our destination must not be divulged to anyone except next of kin, and it must not be mentioned in letters or over the telephone.

In London I stayed at a delightful hostel that had just been opened by the River Plate Committee. At Latin American (Volunteers) House, in Hyde Park Crescent, we could get bed and breakfast in comfortable accommodation for five shillings, with the option of good meals at a reasonable price, and the right to entertain guests. I was glad to meet again friends from my part of the world, and to exchange news. I was impressed and saddened by the length of the Roll of Honour - already. On it were the names of some I had known as schoolboys, and one who had been a fellow traveller only the previous year. A few friends stationed not too far away got special overnight leave to give me a farewell party on my last evening in London. As it happened, some of us were to meet in far away places in the coming years.

* * *

At last we set out, one August evening. Quietly the word was given, and quietly we slipped away from Haslar. Only Miss Waistell saw us off at Portsmouth Harbour, making sure that we carried sandwiches, together with her blessing.

Naval transport awaited us at Waterloo, where our great mountain of luggage - which included a few tennis rackets and golf clubs - invited scornful protests before it was piled on to a couple of lorries, followed by ourselves. Time was pressing! "All aboard? Then hold tight!" and, with caps pulled well down, clinging to the sides and to each other, we made a headlong dash across blacked-out London.

The scene at Euston Station was unforgettable. It seemed that half of Britain must be on the move that night, as harassed officers and NCOs mustered their men, weighed down with equipment and enormous kitbags. This way and that way they were directed, those dazed looking travellers, most of them having no idea where they were going. Clearly there was a large exodus afoot.

The civilian voluntary services were there in force too, performing wonders as they served plentiful hot meals on long trestle tables, working by the dim light of shaded lanterns, and no doubt coping with all sorts of difficulties behind the scenes. When, in the early morning, our slow, overcrowded train was left on a siding for hours, we felt more than ever grateful to the providers of that meal.

At Liverpool, the Monarch of Bermuda was boarded by an ant-like stream of laden, uniformed humanity. Where, one wondered, could so many people be stowed, as unit after unit mounted the gangway and disappeared from view. We, who were to travel in cabins, on an upper deck, had a long wait for our turn in the procession. As we stood, watching and waiting, an Army sergeant came down our line asking for a VAD named Norman. My heart sank. Was I, as an alien, to be turned away at this eleventh hour? But it wasn't so. The officer checking documents had been surprised to discover a Chilean passport, and, indeed, to find that he knew the holder - myself. He had been out in Chile on a short contract with a commercial firm, before the war, and in Concepcion we had played tennis, had picnics and danced at the same gatherings. I was able to give him news of friends, and he seemed surprised to learn how many members of that small British community were currently serving with HM Forces.

That evening, we travelled north to join other ships sheltering in what was probably Gourock - though of course no one would say so. With the soft colours of a northern sunset fading into lingering twilight, it appeared a place of magical beauty and tranquillity.

In the morning the Monarch took her place in a large convoy. We could identify only a few of the ships that made up that great assemblage, but we knew that the Navy was there in strength. To our starboard there was an aircraft-carrier whose little planes flew around reassuringly, and provided thrilling entertainment as they took off and landed on her heaving decks. Our situation was very different from that of the ill-fated Atlantic convoy in which I had travelled the previous year.

Speculating as to our route, we would ask the officers our whereabouts - knowing full well that they could not tell us - but when someone suggested that we might note the colour of the sea, it became clear that we were entering the 'Med.'. The lights of neutral Tangier were glimpsed briefly on our starboard, and in the early morning, acting on a tip from an officer, I managed to steal up on deck in time to look upon the reassuring bulk of Gibraltar on our port. Probably the passage of an Allied convoy through the Mediterranean at the time was unexpected by the enemy. We were not troubled by any action, though later one heard of convoys receiving a good deal of attention from the air.

On that trip we were perhaps the only draft abroad who knew our destination from the start. At points along the way, a stentorial voice would come over the tannoy system: "Draft X ....., prepare to disembark at xxx hours." The ship would make a brief stop, and the people concerned, carrying their hastily packed belongings, would be landed or transferred to another vessel. Our good wishes went with them.

Just before we embarked at Liverpool, our Haslar draft had been joined by a party of nursing sisters and VADs from Scotland and the North of England. With them came an exceedingly keen and energetic Matron. Alas, there was no Red Cross Commandant!

* * *

"Nurse, where are you going?"
"Nurse, get into the shade; you'll get too sunburned, and that is an offence."
"Nurse, where is your brassard?" *(A broad navy-blue armband with a 'Mobile VAD' badge, sometimes discarded in the interest of keeping cool.)*

Soto voce (male) from behind a boat: "Dear me, I thought all nice girls wore bras". The lady was not amused, but others were. It wasn't long before she became known as the Flying Flea, a nickname that followed her through the Service.

It was of course unthinkable that nursing staff should not be fully occupied, and soon the Matron organised an ironing service. Each afternoon a reluctant party of women would descend to the bowels of the ship, and there, standing in the steamy heat, struggle to press great heaps of men's clothing - much to the embarrassment of the owners. This undertaking was fortunately short-lived, because when one woman after another collapsed from the heat and exhaustion, and had to be escorted to the Sick Bay, the Captain put his foot down. In fairness, it must be said that the indefatigable Matron took her turn at the ironing boards.

At daily boat drill we were inspected down to the last detail of our uniform, including the angle of our absurd hats. "It doesn't matter if we're drowned, so long as we die with our hats on", grumbled one exasperated VAD. Many of the offending hats underwent drastic cosmetic surgery on the voyage. Crowns were lowered, brims clipped and curled, so that it is doubtful whether their designers would have recognised them as regulation Red Cross head gear. Many of the white dresses too were given new shapes in the hope that their wearers would look less lumpish.

A number of ships had left the convoy as we proceeded eastward. Alexandria loomed up quite suddenly on our starboard, and we passed so close inshore that it was possible to make out people swimming and others sunbathing along the beach. Soon a sharp turn southward took us into the Suez Canal. It looked unbelievably narrow in places, when it seemed the Monarch had very little room to spare. We made slow progress. Troops stationed along the scorching banks called out in welcome, glad of a chance to talk as we wormed our way through that vulnerable-looking waterway. At Suez we trans-shipped to the Dunera, a regular troopship, again packed like the proverbial sardines.

It was said that in normal times the movement of service personnel through the Red Sea would not be undertaken in the months of July through September. In wartime, with overcrowding and all portholes battened down at sunset in accordance with blackout requirements, conditions were infernal. One would fall asleep, exhausted by the heat, shortly to awake on a bunk saturated with sweat, with matted hair, and with a raging thirst. Those nights seemed endless. We were dependent for air on small, blower type ventilators, and when those failed one night, everyone woke up gasping. Cabin doors were flung open, in defiance of regulations, and the patrols guarding the women's quarters were hard pressed to prevent a stampede to the forbidden decks.

The Captain of the Dunera was a popular man - and deservedly so. Every morning the ship would be turned into the wind for long enough to give everyone a breath of air. After this there would be a scramble to find a quiet corner on deck, where, using a life jacket as a pillow, one might snatch a little sleep before being summoned to boat drill. Conditions improved, and there was tremendous relief when we got into the open waters of the Arabian Sea.

We were sorry to learn that the friendly Dunera would take us no further than Bombay, but we were to remain aboard until we could be transferred to another ship bound for Colombo. During our brief stay, we were granted shore leave, and some of us even late passes. It was exciting to stand beneath the Gateway to India, while planning to see something of Bombay - that teeming city with its blatant poverty and mendacity in the midst of immense wealth and grandeur.

Stepping ashore one would quickly be surrounded by importuning snake charmers, exhibiting their long-suffering cobras, and by ragged beggars who, as darkness fell, would stretch out on the city pavements to spend the night, within a stone's throw of grand shops and luxurious dwellings.

Bombay was at that time full of service personnel, on leave, or awaiting transport to the active theatre of war. There was no lack of volunteers to act as guides for sight-seeing, or as escorts for shopping, and we were reminded of the need to buy white shoes, which had been unavailable in England. The days were all too short, while in the evening one could forget past travel weariness, dining and dancing at the famous Taj Mahal Hotel - all in the spirit of "Hail and Farewell".

For the last stage of our journey we boarded the Cap Touraine, a small and ancient vessel in the service of the Free French, manned by a Lascar crew, and travelling with surely one of the slowest ever convoys - six days from Bombay to Colombo!

Everything on that ship was loathsome. The cabins were dirty; the bunks smelled. The lavatories were filthy, and they had no proper doors. The food was horrible; the bread had weevils. There was no room to walk on the cluttered decks, so that everyone just sat around in a trough of depression, wondering how much longer the voyage would last. It was small wonder that many of our number were suffering from enteritis by the time we arrived.

It was evening when we reached Colombo, thankful to disembark, and hoping for a wash and a decent meal at the hospital VAD quarters. Instead we were rushed to the railway station and packed on to a train, to sit through the night, tired, dispirited, and becoming chilled to the marrow in the early hours, as we wound our way into the hills. Later we could see afresh and rejoice at the beauty of the country we passed through, but on that journey bodily comfort was all that mattered.

On the platform of a wayside station we were greeted by some soldiers returning to Colombo from leave in the hills. They offered us sweets and passed up their water bottles, from which we were grateful to drink. The men were, of course, anxious for news about conditions at home, but we had been long in the limbo of travel and could contribute little.

In the morning, when a jovial Surgeon Captain met us at Diyatalawa station, not everyone was able to appreciate his heartiness, or the rousing music of a welcoming band - though we might have joined our voices in a heartfelt lament!

But this was journey's end. For better or worse it was where we had come of our free will, and where we were likely to remain for a very long time. It would be up to us to adapt and to make the best we could of it.

* * *

Diyatalawa, at about 4,350 feet above sea level, has a relatively temperate climate. It was for years a popular leave centre for service personnel stationed in the Far East, and many will remember it as a place of great beauty, where the nights are cool enough to sleep under blankets. Range upon range of massive hills outlined against a deep blue sky reminded me of the Andes, though of course without the snow, and the sunsets in the hill country are equally magnificent, with the same blue light tingeing the peaks before darkness comes down quite suddenly.

At the time of our arrival there was a brief but violent thunderstorm every afternoon, heralding the monsoon, which we were told would last two to three months. Day by day the periods of rainfall lengthened, until it was wet most of the time, and the temperature dropped sharply at night.

There were brilliant tropical and sub-tropical flowers, including hibiscus, poinsettias, bougainvillea of many colours, mimosa, and canna lilies, besides some that were unfamiliar, but - apart from the delicately perfumed frangipani - most tropical flowers are scentless.

There was also a tempting variety of fruit; pineapples, custard apples, paw-paws, mangoes, mangosteens, tree-ripened citrus fruits, and small, fragrant bananas. All were delicious, though after a time one longed for a crisp, tart apple.

In the early morning there was bird-song, but predominant and persisting throughout the day, there was the harsh squawking of innumerable, repulsive-looking black crows; valuable scavengers these, we were told - but oh, how irritating! However, in time one hardly noticed them.

The village consisted of a straggling row of open-fronted shops, a little bridge across the uncovered drain providing access to each in turn. The dark interiors had little to offer and the prices charged for those scarce goods were exorbitant. Outside, men sat on the pavement, some mending watches, some shoes; others using sewing machines with surprising skill. I never saw women sewing. At the end of the row stood a yellow stucco-fronted building bearing the name Wavell, which did duty as a cinema and also as a chapel. Beyond this again there was a Shell-Mex petrol station with a single yellow and red pump.

We were in the midst of some of the finest tea country and surrounded by large estates. A Scottish great-uncle of mine had once owned a coffee plantation in Ceylon, in the days before a blight destroyed the coffee crops and the planters turned to tea, and he had written a book about his experiences. *(Thirty Years Ago: Coffee Planting In Ceylon, by P D Millie was published in Colombo by A M & J Ferguson, in 1878).* I wondered whether that estate still existed as such, and if we were near it. One soon grew familiar with the dark foliage of the carefully pruned tea bushes and the lighter green of the shade trees set among them, and of tea-pluckers - mostly Tamil women - the huge baskets on their backs suspended from a band across the forehead.

We were warned not to go far afield alone, and no doubt this was sound advice, but how one did long to get away from people, just occasionally! Despite the beauty of its surroundings, Diyatalawa appeared to many as the back of beyond. We soon realised that we would have to make our own life around us.

* * *

Most of us did manage to make a pretty full life for ourselves as time went on. Common interests emerged, and some of the friendships made on foreign service have lasted through the years. There was plenty of social life, and a small officers' club stood conveniently near the hospital gates.

I was surprised and delighted to meet other volunteers from Chile in Diyatalawa from time to time. Soon after our arrival, while buying stamps at the services post office, I turned to find in the queue behind me a young man from

Valparaiso who had also travelled on the Esperance Bay. He was now a Lieutenant RNVR and was taking leave while his ship was in Colombo. We had much news to exchange. And later a WRNS officer, whose family in Santiago were old friends, was sent up on convalescent leave, and liked the place so much that she came again.

The Wavell Cinema provided off-duty entertainment in wet weather. Before settling down to watch some generally ancient film, it was prudent to sprinkle the seats liberally with insecticide powder - a precaution that could save hours of scratching. Bedbugs were everywhere, and no respecters of person.

* * *

We were quartered in a collection of hastily erected, jerry-built huts, divided into 'cabins' of varying sizes. A good deal of manoeuvring went on to secure the best accommodation, and fortunately we were able to make our own arrangements for sharing. The damp in these dwellings was remarkable, especially the first year, before the plaster dried out. Long green whiskers of mildew appeared on shoes and books over night, and the bedding always felt clammy. It wasn't long before some of the huts - including our messroom - were declared unsafe until they received emergency propping. The roofs were just too heavy for the flimsy walls. However, none came down on our heads.

Although the area was not held to be malarial, the use of mosquito nets was compulsory both in hospital wards and in staff living quarters. These nets, suspended from a circular frame, and tucked under the mattress all round, gave at least some illusion of privacy, besides affording protection from the hordes of mosquitoes and other flying and crawling creatures that shared our homes. One learned to shake out shoes before risking ones toes, and often sleeves were found to harbour unwelcome guests. Snakes rarely came in. Even when known to be harmless, they were apt to cause alarm, and all hell was let loose when a cobra was sighted in the hospital grounds.

* * *

Much formality deep-rooted in the nursing hierarchy was soon discarded in hospitals overseas, and starchy traditions that served no useful purpose were swept aside. Of course, VADs lacked the benefit of a full nursing training, but there were situations in which this could be an advantage. Some had joined the service from positions of responsibility that called for initiative and adaptability, and - goodness knows - we were required to improvise and to adapt!

Nor were the VADs the only staff acting in unaccustomed roles. A relatively small number of the nursing Sisters sent out were 'regulars'; most were staff nurses from civilian hospitals, newly promoted to meet wartime needs, and so that experienced QARNNS Sisters could be released to serve in major base hospitals and on hospital ships.

Earlier I believe it had been considered unsuitable to send very young VADs overseas. Our Diyatalawa draft included a number of girls under twenty or twenty-one. They were in fact among the best nurses: responsible as well as adaptable and cheerful.

* * *

RN Hospital Diyatalawa occupied the site of an old Navy rest camp. The wards consisted of long, low, corrugated iron huts set horizontally up a hillside. Between the wards and the wash-houses, 'heads' and sluices there ran a steep, unpaved road which soon became known as Bedpan Alley. During the monsoon, torrents of red-brown water poured down the slope - until this was eventually drained and paved during the last year of my stay.

Patients and nurses posing in 'Bedpan Alley' at RNAH Diyatalawa, 1944.

At the outset we were required to wear regulation white shoes and white cotton stockings, and in these, soaking and discoloured, we waded through the mud. It was quite some time before sufficient red tape could be cut through to permit us to discard stockings and adopt more suitable footwear - sometimes 'Wellingtons'.

For some mysterious reason, despite the monsoon deluge from the skies, there was a chronic shortage of piped water. The supply to the wards and sluices would be cut off without warning for hours at a time, so that unwashed utensils had to be stacked up and dealt with when the flow was restored. This was particularly unfortunate when almost every bed patient suffered from some bowel disorder!

Not only water was scarce. Everything from bedclothes to bedpans was in short supply. Resourcefulness was all-important: the ability to make do with what one could lay hands on. If there were no sheets for that last bed, perhaps it could be made up with mosquito nets, and if there were not enough urine bottles for the early morning specimens, then flower vases or jam jars must do duty. It was surprising how blind some of the administrative staff could be to the lack of equipment - so long as we managed somehow. Certain difficulties and deficiencies were unavoidable - and accepted as such - but many were due simply to red tape and inaction.

* * *

Most of the patients admitted to Diyatalawa Hospital came by hospital train from Colombo, where they had been landed by hospital ship or other means, though a few were men taken ill at local camps. The intake from a hospital train filled every bed and strained our resources; then, as patients recovered - or occasionally died - pressure would decline until the next influx.

It was some time after VJ Day, and shortly before I left Ceylon, that we received a few British POWs released from Japanese camps. The problems of these men were very different. Most had been subjected to physical and mental conditions unimaginable to those who had not shared them, and they wanted no company except each other's. They had struggled to survive and were concerned only with essentials. We did our best for their physical comfort, but asked no questions. A few well-meaning patients who attempted conversation failed to make contact and, at least to begin with, the POWs were left to themselves. But this was not due to lack of sympathy.

A psychiatric ward was opened some time after the hospital was in full swing. It was situated in a separate part of the grounds, and the mentally ill patients were cared for by specially trained SBAs. They were not allowed to join in the life of Bedpan Alley.

There were aspects of the nurse-patient relationship peculiar to such an isolated place as Diyatalawa, where the men received no visitors from outside, and there was little to break the monotony. Our dependence was largely mutual. Many personal problems were brought to us, and we received and welcomed a great deal of practical help. Men who go to sea are for the most part competent and versatile. Willing hands would repair all sorts of equipment that went wrong. They would tinker and coax a flame out of a primus stove that had defied all our efforts; helpless patients were often fed by their more fortunate comrades; and when it was necessary to obtain specimens at regular intervals during the early morning rush period, we were thankful for reliable time checks. Up-patients busied themselves making tea at all hours. This was consumed in incredible quantities, and the ingredients seemed limitless. 'Nurse, here's a cuppa for you' - and, willy-nilly, one accepted a strong and always richly sugared brew.

Discipline was surprisingly good. When trouble did arise, patients and staff joined in trying to smooth things over and save the culprit from disciplinary action. If a convalescent sailor returned from 'shore leave' the worse for beer - or more probably unsuspectedly potent arrack - everyone tried to shield him from detection and the severe consequences of such an offence. And there were other problems to be considered. For instance, nurses must avoid standing in an open doorway or against any light that would reveal too clearly the shape within the white uniform. Occasional fights were inevitable. Generally these were quickly stopped by fellow patients with authority, and the nurse could stand aside. But there were times when such help was not available. I remember one terrifying occasion when, armed with a hastily snatched up pillow, I flung myself between two angry men engaged in a punch-up in the middle of the night. The noise of the rumpus brought help swiftly, and the combatants, abashed and apparently reconciled, were tucked under their mosquito nets just in time for me to report 'All quiet' to the next patrol. When the adrenaline had settled and my knees stopped shaking, I felt sympathetic. What wouldn't one have given at times to 'let off steam' so simply.

It was forbidden to accept gifts from patients, but often these found their way to nurses long after the giver had departed. The choice was usually thoughtful and practical. Many articles of common use were unobtainable in Diyatalawa, including towels, which disappeared from the shops when the 'locals' took to wearing them round their shoulders as 'sweat cloths'. I was touched, as well as grateful when I once received a parcel posted far away and containing a fine towel, accompanied by the laconic message; 'An elephant never forgets.' And who could refuse the offering of a little toy animal made as 'occupational therapy' and thrust into ones hand as a parting gift? We welcomed and shared the news contained in letters from patients, sometimes including photographs taken with the nurses.

Some long-stay patients did fine needlework that would have done credit to any woman. One great bearded seaman spent hours knitting a child's dress in delicate pink. It was, he told me, for a daughter fathered during his last leave and still unknown to him. His next leave would soon be due, and I gathered that the splendid beard was to be another surprise. I hoped it would be appreciated!

Many beards were sacrificed to comfort and hygiene in the tropics. Their very existence was subject to naval discipline. In my early days at Haslar I had been puzzled when I heard a medical officer on his ward round receive a formal request for 'Permission to grow'. This was granted and the fact entered on the case sheet. It entitled the petitioner to start growing a full beard, as an alternative to being clean-shaven. A period in hospital was considered a good time for the transformation, but there must be no unshaved faces except as a preliminary to a respectable beard. So too were bearded sailors required to obtain their officer's 'Permission to shave' before doing so. The Navy must be kept tidy.

It was not unusual to find highly educated men in the ranks. Some had academic qualifications, and some executive skills and experience, and generally they remained non-commissioned from choice - either to see life from a different angle or, as some put it, to let the other chap do the thinking for a change. There was a marked difference in the rank barrier apparent in the Navy and the RAF, with the Army probably coming somewhere in between. At RAF, 'all ranks' entertainment, for instance, one was conscious of an easy camaraderie between officers and men. Perhaps their close association and mutual dependence as aircrews had something to do with this, or perhaps it was just typical of a younger service.

* * *

Many people hated night duty and became exhausted by it - and of course it took its toll. With no separate accommodation for night staff, it was difficult to get enough sleep during the day. At the outset we were assured that there would always be two night nurses on every ward, but before long pressure on the hospital increased, and our numbers were reduced by sickness or other causes, so that any nurse considered capable was required to cope with a forty-bed ward practically unaided. But night duty had many compensations, at least for me; chief among them was escape from a lot of tiresome and often futile routine. There was time to get to know the patients and to study their case histories, and occasionally there was even a chance to read. This was extraordinarily difficult in our daytime herd existence.

Before the ward settled for the night there took place a ceremony typical of the Navy in its formality. It was the Duty Medical Officer's round. As 21.30 hours approached, the nurse flew from bed to bed making sure that all was in order: mosquito nets properly tucked in, and no lighted cigarettes in evidence. Then she called for 'Silence for rounds' - and this had to be absolute; even the bubbling of the steriliser might have to be stifled for this solemn occasion! At the door she received the DMO, escorted by a ward-master and Sister, and reported the number of patients in the ward, any on the dangerous or serious cases lists, as well as any 'boys' (persons under 18). The wardmaster checked numbers with his list; the procession moved on - and tension relaxed. Etiquette satisfied, the DMO would generally return for a cup of tea and the latest gossip at one ward or another, sometimes having to be bundled out by a side entrance if the Matron was reported to be around.

There were ward boys on duty at night, but they were seldom of much help to us. The night was for sleeping - and sleep they did! At the earliest opportunity they would disappear, find a secluded spot on the veranda and, wrapped head and all in a sheet, stretch full length on the 'deck' resisting all efforts to rouse them. It was generally much easier to step over the mummy-like bundle and get on with the job oneself.

The nights were full of strange noises - some of them alarming at first, but less so as one learned to identify the creatures that made them. To begin with there would be a great rustling and flapping as scores of flying foxes, which look like giant bats and are sometimes called fruit bats, took off from the surrounding trees where they had slept, suspended by their feet, throughout the daylight hours. It was as well to be under cover as they passed overhead, their droppings raining down on the tin roofs. The plaintive squealing of tree rats would break through the bass chorus of bull-frogs. On wet nights numbers of small frogs would hop in and out of the wards. These rather endearing visitors were not to be encouraged, because they were said to attract snakes. Time and again would be heard the weird howling of jackals, sometimes sounding quite near. These unlovely scavengers are generally timid, though they were known to venture on to the verandas if their hunger was pressing. Starved looking cats frequented Bedpan Alley, braving jugs of water and other missiles in their foraging and amorous pursuits. Semi-wild dogs (pi-dogs) sometimes strayed in and started fights which sent the alley into uproar. These were too dangerous to approach, best left to their own devices. There were swarms of insects of all kinds, from the incessantly buzzing mosquitoes and a tremendous variety of moths and beetles, to the dainty fire-flies that flitted in and out among the netted beds.

The women's 'loo' was up a steep and lonely hill path, and there was no light when one got up there, so that one imagined spiders or even scorpions lurking in the surrounding gloom, and those essential visits had to be timed so that there was someone available to keep an eye on the ward. The first time I encountered a strange looking man, draped in a blanket and dangling a wooden club, on the path, I was near panic and unable to reply coherently to his greeting. He was only one of the civilian guards patrolling the compound.

There was no break in our twelve-hour period of duty, and of course no chance to get away for a meal. Supper was brought to each ward by a 'runner' - usually a VAD who preferred this quite demanding duty to being the sole nurse on a ward. Besides a welcome meal, the runner carried messages and discussed with the nurses their various needs, so that she could best divide her help among us during the morning rush.

Food was a problem. Eggs were our mainstay, and plenty were provided, but their preparation was full of pitfalls. All the eggs (tiny things) were imported from India - without refrigeration! They were never fresh, and a large proportion frankly 'high', so they could not be boiled. Just one bad egg is enough to spoil an omelette or 'scramble', so that egg by egg scrutiny and a good nose were necessary to avoid disaster. Our mess staff saw to it that we had an alternative in case the worst happened. Tinned soup was the usual reserve standby. It filled one up, but the effect was not lasting on a busy twelve-hour stretch. Cooking called for ingenuity too. At first there were only the primus stoves, but later an ancient wood-burning cooker was installed in a hut at the top of Bedpan Alley. This shelter was also used by the auxiliary night watchmen - usually elderly individuals, who welcomed the warmth as they lay under the table between their rounds, wrapped in an assortment of old blankets and rugs. On wet nights the steam from their clothing would mingle with the aroma of our supper cooking.

* * *

After twenty-eight consecutive nights, we got two days off. Rest was the first consideration, and getting the body's time-clock back to normal sleeping, waking, and eating hours. Equally important it was to get away from the small world of the hospital.

Many of the tea planters offered hospitality to service personnel, and would repeat their invitations to those they found congenial. Some became lasting friends. One tried to return their hospitality, if only in a small measure, by taking as gifts goods that were rationed for civilians, such as liquor, butter, sugar, and even bags of potatoes. Rice too was rationed, although grown in most parts of Ceylon. As the staple diet of a large proportion of the local population, its consumption by Europeans was controlled.

Despite increasing shortages, and staff difficulties, the planters did their best to maintain their traditional way of life - even to the extent of dressing for dinner! Their homes were a haven of comfort and gracious living, and their kindness was much appreciated.

* * *

Soon we came to think nothing of the uncomfortable overnight train journey each way for the sake of a weekend in Colombo, where we could stay at a modest officers' club.

It was in Colombo that I first rode in a rickshaw. My initial reaction was one of pity and revulsion to see a sweating, panting man running between the shafts on bare feet. However, one soon learned that the rickshaw men did this from choice and that they earned a lot of money. Certainly they charged us exorbitant fares, until we learned something of the ways of the East and the age-old art of haggling.

Saturday nights were festive at the Galle Face Hotel, where one saw officers' uniforms of all the services, and a fine array of decorations. But through that scene of gaiety there ran a sombre thread. Ceylon provided bases for intensive training in jungle warfare *(the whereabouts and purpose of bases such as Horana, and the exploits of Force 136 and the like were, of course, shrouded in secrecy),* and it was the point of departure for special units proceeding to Burma, so that ones friends or dancing partners might be on special leave before going into action.

One such friend was a fellow volunteer from Chile, at the time a Captain in the Lancashire Fusiliers. Our plans to meet had fallen through repeatedly because his leave would be cancelled at the last minute. When granted, it was brief - and final. On Saturday we swam, we danced, exchanging news from home as we made plans for Sunday. In the morning he was recalled, and I knew there could be no direct news. Later I learned through the River Plate Committee that he had been reported 'Missing', and later 'Killed in Action'. That word 'Missing' - what grim possibilities it conjured up!

I had interesting leaves in Kandy and various places of interest with another VAD named Joyce who I had met at Haslar and had shared a cabin with on the voyage out.

* * *

I suppose for all of us, everywhere, the impact of events is largely measured by distance. To many people in Britain who had no relatives or close friends serving in the Far East, the Japanese campaign must have seemed remote. Fast moving events in North Africa, and then in Europe, had thrust the Eastern War right out of the headlines, where it had never received much of a share anyway. And so, with the collapse of Nazi Germany, and the liberation of occupied countries in Europe, it seemed the war was over, and it was time to celebrate: understandably so.

But in Southeast Asia there was as yet no peace, either for the 'Forgotten Army' in Burma, or for the thousands of interned civilians. We knew only a little about the sufferings of the troops bogged down in jungle warfare, and of course no one could visualise the horrors of the prison camps. Men who came to Ceylon on brief leave from time to time looked worn and aged beyond their years. They savoured each day and each small comfort, talking little of that to which they must return - though afterwards some would write more revealingly.

When, on May 8th 1945, arrangements were announced for holding celebrations in Diyatalawa to mark VE-Day, many of us felt that wild jubilation was premature and out of place. Rejoice one did - but there was still a long way to go.

* * *

Later in May I was one of a party of VADs transferred to temporary duty in Colombo. This was a routine move designed to give the Colombo nurses a change to the healthier climate of the hills. After our rather circumscribed life in Diyatalawa, the change was generally welcome, with the prospects of better shops and a more sophisticated social life. It was time we had a move anyway.

At that time the Navy occupied available accommodation in different parts of the Colombo General Hospital. This was a straggling building and, although the naval wards were separate from the civilian, we shared the same approaches. Escorting a patient from one department to another, for instance, one might run into a party of saffron-robed Buddhists priests, or perhaps a class of Sinhalese medical students following their chief on his rounds. These young men would look at us with curiosity mingled with disdain, their stethoscopes always displayed prominently so that there could be no doubt as to their status. There was a good deal of anti-British feeling in Ceylon just then, particularly among the young 'leftist' elements, and although it was no great distance from the hospital to our quarters, we were advised to keep together and to call for an escort when coming off duty after dark. I recall only one unpleasant encounter, when a few of us were stopped and harangued by a party of young men whom we took to be students.

The work at Colombo was on the whole interesting, with more surgery and more acute cases than were generally admitted at Diyatalawa, and the hospital was somewhat better equipped. While there I gained a little experience in two aspects of nursing that were new to me.

While on night duty on an officers' ward, my patients included a number of supposedly 'safe' psychiatric cases waiting to be invalided home. These troubled men shared a deep fear of being 'shut away' on their return, and some had definite ideas of escape. One particularly likeable and gentle patient gave me some bad moments. I was writing at the desk one night and did not hear him come up behind me on bare feet. Suddenly I felt my shoulders grasped, and he said 'Come on nurse, it's time for us to go over the roof'. We were on a first floor, and at right angles to the veranda was the sloping glass roof of a covered way. This was clearly my patient's objective, towards which I was being gently but firmly propelled. Of course there was no real danger. If I had called for help loudly enough some other patient would have come to my assistance, but one did not want to cause a disturbance or, above all, to distress the already worried Mr W. "I don't think it's a very nice night; it looks like rain", I faltered, thinking desperately of the 'dos' and 'don'ts' in which I had been so briefly instructed. "Shall we wait until there's a moon?". Slowly the pressure on my shoulders relaxed; a resigned voice said, "Yes, nurse, perhaps tomorrow." - and I got the troubled wanderer back to his bed before reaching for the telephone to a Sister on the floor below. Following this experience the patient was more adequately sedated at night, and later a second nurse joined me on the ward. After I had completed my night duty I learned that Mr W was being transferred to the psychiatric ward in Diyatalawa. I hoped that he might escape being 'shut away' for long, which he so greatly feared.

* * *

The fecundity of the East was manifest. That old hospital building teemed with animal and insect life, including hordes of cockroaches, and repulsive, pinkish-skinned rats. Scraggy, long-legged cats would dart out from unexpected corners and streak past one legs, and then their eyes would gleam eerily from some point of vantage. Of course the cats were meant to prey on the rats, but they were just no match for these. Sad-looking mongrel dogs skulked around in the hope of scraps, yelping if anyone raised a hand, as though they feared a missile. One night a hideous din was traced to a water supply tank into which a pi-dog had fallen. It took several 'boys', armed with a ladder and with brooms, to rescue the terrified animal, and of course by this time the whole ward was awake. I never knew what - if anything - was done about the water in that tank!

With a high incidence of typhoid in Ceylon, all drinking water was boiled - or supposed to be. We would leave our empty bottles outside the 'galley' before meals, and pick up refilled ones on our way out. The water was never really cold; it was flat and tasted horrible, but one needed to drink a lot in that heat, and we carried the bottles with us when we went on duty, leaving them on window-sills or on lockers while working. (There were no canteens or machines dispensing iced drinks in those days!). And it was no good worrying too much about hygiene. Carrion crows often flew into our mess, settling on uncovered dishes of fruit or bread. Only when they saw us coming would one or two 'boys' detach themselves from their chattering huddle and flap a cloth ineffectually at the birds.

Indoors the sticky heat was made bearable by large ceiling fans. Geckoes - small, semi-transparent lizards - ran up and down the walls and across the ceilings, apparently impervious to gravity, though sometimes, caught by the blade of a fan, one would be hurled onto a unsuspecting head. However, the geckoes were much more welcome than the multitude of insects on which they fed, each flick of their prehensile tongues sounding like a miniature whiplash.

* * *

I stayed in Colombo for about three months, and I was there when the Japanese surrender was precipitated by the atom bomb.

Few people can have felt more cut off from the world than those fighting and those stationed in Southeast Asia. Relief that the war in Europe was over, and that they might have homes to go back to if they survived, was followed by the expectation of a long-drawn-out struggle against the Japanese. Men in the forces were understandably sceptical about promised reinforcements that would turn the tide; they had waited too long. And then - at first whispered with bated breath, but quickly confirmed with authority - came the news that a bomb of unheard of destructive power had been dropped on Japan. Whatever the ultimate consequences of that horror, the war was over this time.

On the night of August 15th every hotel and place of entertainment opened its doors to all ranks, and people flocked into Colombo from far and near. I celebrated at the Galle Face Hotel, with friends who came down from Diyatalawa for the occasion. The mood of jubilation was irresistible. The bands blared. We danced, we sang, we toasted each other and the future as we shared briefly in that fragile bubble of euphoria. It was a never-to-be-forgotten scene, and dawn had broken over the Galle Face Green before that party came to an end.

* * *

Of course the ending of the war brought no immediate change to our service prospects. There would be no fresh casualties due to enemy action, but wounds did not heal at once; tropical diseases would continue to take their toll as long as service personnel remained in the area, and many released prisoners of war would require hospital treatment before they were fit enough to be sent home.

One change did take immediate effect, for which we were thoughtlessly unprepared: the small addition to our pay described as 'Japanese campaign war risks allowance' was - not surprisingly - stopped forthwith.

* * *

In October 1945 a home-bound ship was due to leave Colombo carrying hundreds of women entitled to priority release from the services. Among them was a party of VADs granted compassionate discharge for health and family reasons.

* * *

Our draft had been in Ceylon for over two years, which was longer than usual for a posting in the tropics. The demobilisation of VADs was dependent on length of service as well as age, and I knew that my group was not due for release before April or May 1946. With no family in England, I was not anxious to return months ahead of my discharge, and so - in common with a few of my colleagues - I submitted a request for transfer, to serve the remainder of my time in the Navy at any other Southeast station.

I don't think any of us felt very optimistic about the chances of a move, especially as time went by. Then, late in November '45, as I checked in at midnight after weekend leave, I was handed an urgent message: I was to be ready to leave the following day for Colombo, en route to Singapore, by air.

Frenzied packing was followed by the briefest round of good-byes, and then a

by Alice Brereton-Smith nee Ruttledge.

hastily assembled farewell drinks party at the medical mess. One of the doctors there quickly decided that he had business in Colombo that very afternoon, and he would take me down by road. Perhaps it was the effect of pink gin, coupled with the thought of leaving such good friends, but I had to swallow a great big lump in my throat as we were waved through the hospital gates. In that remote place we had shared many experiences, both good and bad, and together we had fought our battle against Red Tape - generally achieving our ends.

* * *

From the urgency of my departure it might have been supposed that I would immediately be put on a plane taking me to vital work in Singapore. As an old stager familiar with the vagaries of service postings, it came as no great surprise to find that nobody in Colombo had heard of me or of any draft to Singapore. I had outstripped the 'signal'. However, it caught up with me the following day, and the draft included two VADs from St Peter's Hospital, Colombo, where I was to join them until we left. We were instructed to 'stand by' for early departure. We stood! Days went by. They became a week; then a fortnight. When we ventured to ask whether any date had been arranged for our departure, we were told that it was none of our business; the Sister in charge had the matter well in hand. But we had our doubts, and at last we approached RAF Transport Command ourselves, only to learn that no proper application for our passages had ever been made! At the hospital we were received with stern disapproval - but also some red faces - when we produced the necessary documents and asked that they might be signed.

And so, at last, a few days before Christmas 1945, we boarded an RAF Sunderland

Flying Boat. These craft were based at Koggala, on a secluded and enchantingly beautiful little inlet. It was midnight when we went aboard, and my last sight of Ceylon was a brilliantly moonlit panorama of coconut palms and phosphorescent waves breaking on a crescent of white sand.

* * *

I think it would be obvious to any mechanically minded person - which I am not - that tremendous power is needed to lift a huge, heavily laden machine out of the water. I had not imagined anything so shattering. Surely the whole structure must come apart under its own power in that mammoth travail, but at least we came unstuck and lumbered off - all in one piece.

It was a far from restful night. The other two women lay on benches along either side of a table. I had a 'li-lo' in a small deck space fore. The body of the plane was full of troops. Time and again my air bed became deflated, and the deck grew harder and harder. Every time the crew made tea I was given a cup, and there was much to-ing and fro-ing. The route to the 'loo' might have been designed for an obstacle race! In the morning I volunteered to help get breakfast. Baked beans on toast, tea and bread and butter may sound an easy enough menu, but in a galley space about three feet by five, and with everything rocking, it was quite an undertaking; yet those RAF crews must have provided similar breakfasts for every planeload of personnel they carried. By the time plate and mugs had been handed down a human conveyor belt and everyone fed, we were hovering over the Penang Channel, where we were to put down to re-fuel, quite close to a familiar liner of the Valparaiso/Liverpool run. The island of Penang looked so beautiful from the air that I decided to try and get back there some time - and this I did a couple of months later.

* * *

At Singapore I was delighted to find two ex-Haslar VADs - Helen and Judy - who had travelled out with our Ceylon draft in 1943 and had been nursing at Trincomalee. They had arrived by sea a few weeks earlier with a party of WRNS and a Sister, and had set up a WRNS sick bay.

The day after our arrival we newcomers set out to see a little of Singapore. In the foyer of Raffles Hotel I asked a pleasant looking woman if she knew whether we could get lunch there. When she heard that we were VADs she beamed upon us; we were to be guests of herself and her sister, and they would take no refusal. These ladies introduced themselves as Elsie and Doris Waters - alias Gert and Daisy, the comediennes, touring with ENSA. It was past the usual lunch hour and, at a time of many shortages, the head waiter regretted that all he could offer us was corned beef hash. It was delicious. Served with the traditional perfection of the Raffles, and in such good company, it was a memorable meal, and after it we lingered over coffee in our hostesses' room while they related some of their experiences, being their thoroughly charming and entertaining selves.

The artists who went abroad with ENSA did a great service. Some of us had been fortunate enough to see John Gielgud in Hamlet while in Colombo, and I had also enjoyed some good concerts, but of course it was comedy and review that had the widest popular appeal among the forces. Some of the artists were hard hit by different climates and conditions. A few had turned up in Diyatalawa to seek treatment at the hospital for a variety of ills, while continuing on their tours regardless.

In the afternoon we sent off telegrams to our homes. Later I learned that a message I had handed in about 4 p.m. had been received in Santiago early that same morning - so great was the difference in time.

On enquiring about tea we were directed to a NAAFI canteen. Here I was surprised to see a woman volunteer from Chile who had been a fellow passenger on the Esperance Bay in 1942. She greeted me with typical Latin American exuberance. I had heard that she was serving in the WAAF, but I could not identify the uniform she was now wearing. Apparently she had transferred to one of the many auxiliary services that sprang up towards the end of the war and proliferated in accordance with Parkinson's Law. Probably each of these sub-services complemented another service, but I found the string of letters on their shoulder 'flashes' just too difficult to interpret or to remember.

I lost my heart to Singapore at first sight, and I was not disappointed on closer acquaintance. There was a sense of timelessness about that city and its people, who had so recently been liberated from enemy occupation, with its indignities and disruption of their way of life. It was said that there had been a good deal of 'accommodation' with the occupying forces, and of bending before the wind of circumstance. Be that as it may, four months later life in Singapore appeared surprisingly normal, and of course a strong and efficient administration did much to hasten its recovery.

At high tide the Singapore River was a hub of activity and a beguilingly attractive sight, packed with craft of all kinds, and enlivened by sails of many colours. But soon one learned that distance lent enchantment. It was well to retreat prudently before the tide went out, leaving behind refuse of every description, to rot in the shallows and give off smells that could better be imagined than described.

Many of the streets appeared as if beflagged, with clothes threaded on long poles sticking out of the windows to dry. The street signs were in English as well as in Chinese characters. There were stalls everywhere selling cooked food, some of which looked and smelled very appetising, but service personnel were forbidden to eat anything offered outside approved canteens. It was believed that a lot of poisoned food had been left behind by the Japanese.

The women, wearing neat trousers and high-necked tunics, carried their babies astride their hips. Tidy, well-behaved children looked like dolls, except that - as with most Eastern children - their eyes were too old and much too wise.

* * *

My introduction to the social life of Singapore was a happy one. Helen, having heard that I would probably arrive before Christmas, had accepted on my behalf an invitation to dine at an RE officers' mess on Christmas Eve, and to go out carol singing with them afterwards. This expedition had been planned thoughtfully so as to give pleasure to some of the people who had suffered long captivity in Japanese camps.

After so good a dinner that we could not possibly have taken a really deep breath, thirteen of us set out in two army jeeps. We were three women in the party, and on arrival at each house we sang the first verse of a carol alone - just to reassure any nervous occupants. Our welcome was overwhelming. People who had recently returned to what was left of their homes were touchingly pleased. One middle aged couple came out to greet us walking carefully on their new artificial limbs; each had lost a leg while in the prison camps, but they were happy to be alive and together again. Some people said they had lost hope of ever seeing another Christmas. At every stop we were regaled with refreshments - alcoholic or otherwise. Towards the end of our round we called on the C-in-C Singapore, where we joined briefly in a rather formal party. And finally we dropped in on the American Consul. Here a party of homesick men received us warmly, their rumpled hair suggesting that they had pulled on vests hurriedly when they heard women's voices. We made quite a long stay with the Americans, and indeed by this time we were completely hoarse.

I have never been much good at singing, but pouring out those familiar carols in the tropical night on that first post-war Christmas was something I shall never forget.

And memorable too was the midnight service in St. Andrew's Cathedral. As late arrivals, room was somehow made for us in the packed congregation gathered to hear the Christmas message of goodwill and forgiveness, pronounced by the Bishop of Singapore, himself a survivor of internment by the Japanese.

* * *

Christmas over, we began to wonder what next? Presumably we had been sent to Singapore to nurse - or had we? The small WRNS sick bay was adequately staffed by a Sister and two VADs. There was no naval hospital ashore, and the hospital ship Gerusalemme, anchored out at sea, was undoubtedly staffed by Sisters and sick berth attendants; VADs did not serve on ships. Indeed it was a mystery why the last three of us had been sent to Singapore at all.

After a time I was added to the staff of a small out-patient clinic at SEAC (South-East Asia Command) Headquarters in Cathay Building. Here one medical officer, assisted by one SBA and myself, dealt with such minor ills as perhaps a brigadier's boil, an ATS officer's sprained ankle, or somebody's ingrowing toenail. It was all quite pleasant and undemanding. It hardly seemed to justify my urgent transfer by air!

One morning there came into the clinic a very senior naval officer - clearly a man of outstanding personality and, I felt sure, possessed a keen sense of humour. He stopped and talked, asking me a number of questions about my work experience, while watching me syringe a patient's ear. (I didn't think he altogether approved of my method!). The next morning I was summoned to the office of the Medical Division of SEAC and was appointed Acting PA to one of the Navy's ablest and most distinguished medical officers. Among his many important functions, Surgeon-Captain Rainsford (the late Surgeon-Rear-Admiral S G Rainsford, CB, RN) was medical adviser to the Supreme Allied Commander; he was Head of the Naval Tropical Research Unit, and was currently engaged in a considerable research project. I felt grateful to the staff of the Pathological Department in Diyatalawa who, knowing of my interest, had given me a opportunity to learn a little about the work in that fascinating field, inviting me to see diagnostic tests, showing me interesting findings under the microscope etc. What I had learned in the Path. Lab. proved very helpful in enabling me to cope with my new and demanding job. The terminology was particularly important, as I found myself confronted with a great mass of material concerning different aspects of research, and which it became my immediate duty to sort out and index.

Apart from the research project, the functions of the Medical Division were wide, and included epidemiological control in Southeast Asia, hygiene for the troops, assessment of nutrition levels in camp diets, liaison with welfare bodies etc. Not only was the work tremendously interesting, and my relations with the whole department of the happiest, but I felt that this experience might sharpen my wits and prepare me for earning my living once more in competitive civilian life. This was a matter which had occupied my mind increasingly as the time for my discharge and repatriation approached.

* * *

The food situation was difficult. Certainly we in the Services never went short, but there was a lack of fresh food, and menus were generally monotonous. It takes an inspired cook to make appetising meals in large quantities, especially when the ingredients are dehydrated, though some of the messes at which we were guests seemed to achieve wonders. Apart from NAAFI run establishments, the Tanglin Club (officers in the services enjoyed the facilities of the Tanglin Club by courtesy of its civilian members), and Raffles Hotel (which had maintained a remarkably high standard through all vicissitudes), service personnel were forbidden to eat at restaurants - and this probably saved a lot of sickness.

Vitamin tablets were issued to everybody, as well as salt tablets to counteract the effect of excessive sweating. Mepacrine was given as a prophylactic against malaria, though some people refused to take it because it makes the skin yellow.

* * *

For women stationed in Singapore the social round was never-ending, and to many this period represented a last fling before returning as strangers to an inclement world. No evening was spent in quarters unless from choice or duty obligations. We dined and danced at clubs, messes, and aboard ships, sometimes crossing the famous causeway to visit stations on the mainland. At Johore Bahru the Sultan's Palace had been opened as an officers' club. It provided spacious comfort both indoors and out, and had many interesting features. Wandering in the grounds I was introduced to an unusual pet; a tame and friendly zebra.

A curfew was imposed after some New Year jollifications had got out of hand. All service vehicles had to be off the roads by 1 am. Minutes before the hour a roar could be heard as fleets of cars, jeeps or other vehicles changed gear to take the bend and climb a steep rise before depositing their women passengers at Ardmore Flats, and speeding for home, with never a minute to spare. Life at Ardmore Flats was never dull; it was far from luxurious! with one bathroom to be shared by fifteen women, and all the sanitary fittings contained in the same four walls, there was clearly no chance of privacy. Plenty of goodwill and a sense of humour were essential to avoid friction.

With no laundry facilities, we could not have managed without the services of an 'amah', usually shared between two or three of us. Before leaving for work in the morning, one left on the foot of the bed the clothes worn the previous day - including long evening dresses - knowing that on return everything would be back, beautifully laundered by those small, skilful hands. The 'amahs' certainly earned their modest pay as well as our appreciation.

* * *

One Sunday Judy and I were invited to a sailing picnic by some senior naval officers who had the use of a patrol launch. We cruised out to sea for some distance before coming to the so-called Thousand Islands. These are of all shapes and sizes, and some of them are magically beautiful, with sandy white beaches and waving coconut palms. Navigation among them is hazardous owing to projecting reefs, which are difficult to see until one is right upon them. We were making for a particularly lovely island which our hosts had discovered earlier, when suddenly a bump and an ominous grating noise warned us that we were aground on a coral reef. There was nothing for it but to wait for the tide to float us off in its own good time. On our port side the water was shallow, and the sea bed presented a fascinating scene; coral of many colours and fantastic shapes, among which swam multicoloured fishes - some tiny jade ones and others orange and yellow, followed by larger angel fish striped in heavenly blue, green and silver. There were also some rather repulsive, snake-like creatures, with tentacles at one end, and masses of water beetles wriggling along at great speed. We lay on our stomachs poking about with boat-hooks and exploring this submarine world, until the heat became unbearable; then - not without misgivings - we went over the side into deep water to starboard. I kept close in, because, however beautiful, I was shy of the water population, but Judy and one of the men swam to another island and brought back a large coconut. The milk was delicious, especially when laced with rum.

Today, exotic tropical fishes are to be seen in aquariums everywhere, while intrepid skin divers and sophisticated colour photography have made the underwater world a familiar sight, but we were entranced to see those colourful creatures in their natural habitat at such close quarters.

We had our picnic under an awning on deck - and an absolute banquet it was. Well-iced drinks were followed by cold roast duck, crisp salads, fruit, cheese, and excellent coffee, all perfectly served by the versatile 'crew' in the role of steward. The tide did not lift us off for several hours, and we got in as the sun was setting, with a soft pink light tinting the sails of the junks, and the buildings in the harbour appearing phantom-like above the evening haze.

Not everyone could offer such lavish hospitality, but there were many good picnics and worthwhile expeditions. Once we drove about thirty miles into the Malay mainland and explored an abandoned rubber estate. A fine house was in a sad state of dilapidation, but the overgrown garden still bloomed, and we picked armloads of flowers for the sick bay. Then we swam in a pool with a crystal stream flowing through it. What, one wondered, had become of the family whose home it had been?

* * *

One expedition was made in the spirit of a pilgrimage, and it left haunting memories. The place had been named Victory Hill. A plain wooden cross marked the spot where a handful of Australians had made a last stand, in 1942. As prisoners, weakened by sickness and malnutrition, they had been forced to build a road and steps to the summit, being cut down one by one as they fell exhausted.

* * *

Exploration of outlying quarters of Singapore was sometimes rewarding. One day Helen and I came upon an extraordinary-looking garden, full of artificial hillocks, grottoes and towers, with dragons, life-size deer, storks and other animals and birds scattered about. The gate was guarded by a benign looking Sikh, and we asked him if we might have a look round. He seemed glad to show us an exquisite miniature village, complete with little temples, bridges, and kiosks, peopled with tiny human and animal figures. There was a hotchpotch of childishly amusing, and some quite hideous objects, and it was all rather like a Walt Disney fantasy.

Our guide then suggested that we might like to see over the house, which he told us contained many treasures. We hesitated when we heard that the owners were in residence, but everyone bowed and smiled as we went in, and we were shown around by courteous servants. In an otherwise unremarkable, and indeed ugly house, there were numberless cabinets full of ornamental figures in jade, alabaster, cornelian, rose quartz, and many different stones which we were unable to identify. The treasures were displayed all over the house, even in the bedrooms. There were far too many items crowded together to allow a proper appreciation, but there were some lovely things, and the wealth contained in that collection alone must have been enormous.

Later we learned that the house belonged to Au Boon Par and Au Boon Haw, eccentric millionaire brothers who had, years ago derived, and continued to amass a huge fortune from the sale of an ointment labelled Tiger Balm. The secret formula was said to embody some of the legendary qualities of the tiger, and all sorts of unlikely benefits were claimed from its use. We had, in fact, stumbled upon a mere fragment of the fabulous Tiger Balm empire, which years later extended its scope to a number of enterprises, some of which featured in a much publicised legal wrangle.

* * *

There were different pleasures to be enjoyed. Besides the various forms of entertainment provide by ENSA, some excellent concerts were given by the Singapore Symphony Orchestra, composed of gifted and enthusiastic musicians of many races, and ably conducted by Dr. Eric Chisholm. On release from internment that remarkable Scot had lost no time in getting together other survivors and re-forming the orchestra, even while some of its members appeared pitifully frail and emaciated. Their performances always filled the Victoria Hall to capacity and we counted ourselves lucky when we were able to join those wonderfully appreciative audiences.

* * *

Once, on the outskirts of Singapore, I was horrified to see some old Chinese women hobbling along on grotesque little stumps of feet, and later I saw them bathing their feet in a stream. I had never seen the result of foot binding, nor had I given it much thought, but I had believed the practice to have been abandoned generations ago. Apparently this was not so, and I was told that some women actually favoured this traditional mutilation.

* * *

Shopping in Singapore - as in most Eastern cities - was a lengthy process, and best not undertaken until one had learned something of the art of bargaining and had time at ones disposal. There were, in the best quarters, eminently high class shops, where dealings in fine quality goods were conducted with dignity and dispatch, and where anything in the nature of haggling would be unthinkable. But in the general run of shops no one was expected to pay the first price asked. There would be a series of offers and counter offers, with the customer walking out, followed by a persuasive shopkeeper, until a compromise was reached without too much loss of 'face' by either party. The asking price would of course vary according to the customer's appearance and presumed standing. Officers soon learned to remove their badges of rank, and women - if not in uniform - to wear their simplest dress to go shopping. Some Europeans had scant patience with this age-old custom, but they generally came off the losers. I found a good method was to look the shopkeeper in the eye and ask him what he would have to say if his wife paid so much for the article. This usually fetched a laugh and a quick drop in price.

There was much business rivalry between the Malay merchants and the hard-headed Chinese, who learn to drive a bargain at a very early age.

Bartering with the civilian population was frowned upon by the authorities, but no active steps were taken to prevent it. The demand for cigarettes was unfailing, and most non-smokers were glad to exchange their ration for something that would be of use to them. I never heard of any dire consequences.

* * *

My annual leave had been due some time before I left Ceylon, but I had not applied for it. The hospital was short-staffed at the time and, for my part, I wanted to be available if the hoped for transfer came through.

It was now February '46. Helen was also due leave, and we decided that this was almost certainly our last chance to see something more of the East. We were particularly anxious to visit Bangkok, and we had a friend there, a medical officer ex-Diyatalawa - who had assured us of a good time.

Despite my recent arrival, Surgeon-Captain Rainsford approved my leave and authorised my travel papers. However, Helen's requisition had to go through different channels, and Bangkok was disallowed: Thailand had been declared out of bounds for service personnel on leave. This was a blow indeed, but we did not give up hope. We decided to go to Penang - which I wanted to visit anyway - and, once away from Singapore, we thought there might be ways and means. We were prepared to try. Before we left I hinted that I might get to Bangkok, and I felt that my boss was not unsympathetic.

We travelled on an RAF Dakota (Douglas DC 3) with 'bucket' seats facing each other down the sides. We were given blankets and 'Mae Wests' and, in case we had to 'ditch', instructed to place our arms round each others shoulders to lessen the shock of impact. On one side of me there sat a frightfully smelly and fierce looking Jat soldier, so I hoped that closer contact would not be necessary.

The Dakota put us down at Butterworth, on the mainland, and from there we took a channel ferry to Georgetown, capital of the island of Penang. We had made no advance booking, and had been warned that we might have difficulty in finding accommodation. However, we were lucky to get into the Runnymede Hotel, which was being run as a sort of officers' hostel, and was therefore not expensive.

At breakfast on our first morning we were intrigued to see a dignified head waiter approach each table in turn and proffer two small dishes. We wondered what special delicacy he was serving with such ceremony, and whether we too would be favoured. Yes, our turn came: one dish contained vitamin tablets and the other Mepacrine. He watched us swallow them too!

Penang was just as beautiful as it had looked to me while flying over it in the Sunderland, with gentle outlines and soft colours. The vegetation looked lush, with many lovely trees. Tea, rubber, rice, and coconuts seemed to thrive, and there was a great variety of fruits.

There were few visible scars of war. The hasty, unplanned evacuation in December '41 took place after a single Japanese air-raid, and valuable crops, as well as tin-smelting machinery, had been abandoned intact, proving of great value to the enemy. The small amount of bomb damage apparent was, we were told, caused by Allied raids during the final stages of the war. All the main buildings seemed to be concentrated in and around Georgetown, with only small villages and isolated houses - many built on stilts - stretching beyond. We were surprised to see street lighting, which was absent in Singapore, and plenty of tricycle 'rickshaws'.

The beaches are a bather's paradise, with shady trees, rocks, and firm white sand stretching for miles. Opposite the Swimming Club there was an area protected from sharks by a wooden palisade, and, for those who preferred it, a sizeable swimming pool. But, however lovely, tropical beaches hold unexpected hazards. One perfect-looking morning, just as we were about to enter the sea, the sun vanished and the sky darkened dramatically; a storm blew up with incredible suddenness: forked lightening flashed, while torrential rain and a fierce wind lashed the bay into a turmoil in a matter of minutes, during which we crouched in the shelter of some rocks. Then the storm passed as quickly as it had come, and the sea was soon as calm as a mill-pond. We ventured in.

We were shown round Penang by a charming Chinese family, introduced by mutual friends in Singapore. With them, we boarded a funicular railway that took us to the top of Penang Hill, which is nearly 3,000 feet high. It was a holiday, and the carriages were packed to about three times their normal capacity, but no one seemed to worry, and the view from the summit was certainly rewarding. Later we visited a Chinese temple, where a Buddhist festival was being celebrated with the beating of huge leather drums and the ringing of massive, deep-toned bells. After this I was not surprised when we were invited to feed the temple turtles.

Horse racing seemed an unlikely pursuit in such surroundings, but Georgetown had a racecourse, and our host was devotee and owner. The horses we were shown looked absolute thoroughbreds, and were beautifully groomed. It seemed remarkable how very quickly the people of this and other eastern countries had put behind them the horrors of war, and gone back to their normal way of life.

We were also invited to a Chinese circus. It was an interesting experience, though we were unable to appreciate much of it. One of the highlights was an excellent but blood-freezing performance by a troupe of acrobats from Shanghai.

The next morning we were able to explore the countryside at leisure, marvelling at the variety of wild flowers and gorgeous butterflies.

Penang remains an enchanting memory. *(Inevitably that lovely island has long since been 'discovered' and exploited by the tourist industry, and it now boasts towering hotels and a bustle of motor traffic).*

* * *

While enjoying all this we were planning our next move. Rangoon, with its famous pagodas was our immediate aim. It was not on our approved itinerary, but neither was it 'out of bounds'. The RAF had seats on a Dakota, and no one asked to see our papers.

* * *

It was late afternoon when we came down over a brown, arid-looking land. The huge aerodrome was packed with machines of all kinds. The air was dry and dusty - a marked change from the humidity of Singapore. Apart from the runways, the ground was rough and full of potholes - evidence of the battles that had raged back and forth in some of the fiercest fighting of the war for possession of the field. Despite all difficulties, the RAF provided welcome tea and sandwiches in a clean waiting room.

Evening approached and, again with no booking, we were fortunate to get a couple of beds on a landing at a YWCA hostel. This was rather primitive, with lavatories of the ground level kind, and water to be scooped out of an Ali Baba type stone jar and poured over oneself as a shower or bath. It was the dry season, but the temperature dropped sharply at night. In the morning we awoke to the raucous squawking of crows - reminiscent of Ceylon.

Rangoon was a scene of ruin and desolation. The city was reduced to heaps of rubble, and one got the impression that everything had stood still in the six months since the war ended. The streets, pitted with holes and deep in dust, would doubtless became a morass when the rains came. The facades of fine buildings - many still bearing nameplates - gaped across at the ruins opposite. Among all the desolation, and within sight of our hostel, stood a graceful little pagoda, its pinnacle covered in gold leaf. The Allies had, in their bombing, spared the temples wherever possible.

There was no transport problem - at least for white women. One had only to step out of the door for a service vehicle of some kind to draw up and its driver to offer a lift - anywhere! Our first rescuer was a Captain RE driving a jeep. The captain took us to his mess where we were joined by other officers and taken to the Yacht Club for some very pleasant sailing. Other invitations followed, and later we were entertained at the fine Gymkhana Club, but that afternoon we had an important engagement of our own: a visit to the famous Shwedagon Pagoda.

The lofty golden spire of this temple dominates the city from a hilltop, and it is the only part visible as one approaches. Inside the precincts - where we left our shoes on entering - we climbed a long flight of steps with stalls on either side selling goods to raise funds for the upkeep of the temple. I stopped and bought a decorative brass rice spoon, which I have treasured ever since. The sight at the top is breath-taking. The huge central pagoda, with its long, slender pinnacle covered entirely in gold leaf, and wearing a circlet of bells, is surrounded by a host of smaller spires and turrets, in marble, lacquer and gold leaf. The entire vane is studded with precious and semi-precious stones. It is a dazzling sight in every way, and we saw it at the best time, with the late afternoon sun enhancing and blending the many colours, and a gentle breeze swaying the little bells.

In that short time one could take in only a fraction of the carvings, the lines of the buildings, and the beauty of the awe-inspiring whole, but I am thankful to have seen what is surely the loveliest of the Burmese pagodas.

* * *

Burma was not a country in which to linger on holiday. It was a ravaged land, and haunted by memories of friends who had not returned.

We had little opportunity to meet any Burmese. The few women with whom we came in contact at the YWCA hostel - while not unfriendly - seemed more reserved than most of the other Orientals whom we had met.

Outside Rangoon we saw camps occupied by troops - white and coloured - just waiting to be taken home. Wandering among their tents, they looked bored and depressed. Presumably the civilian administration could make no use of them; yet there was much work to be done in Rangoon.

* * *

Helen and I decided to put our luck to the test once more, and the next day we called at the RAF Booking Centre. Yes, there were seats on a plane going to Bangkok - but we must get authority from the Navy! We submitted our papers with bated breath. No one seemed to have heard of any ban on Thailand, or, if they had, they were not concerned. And so, on February 16th, we boarded yet another Dakota.

* * *

In my childhood the names Bangkok and Baghdad had a ring of fairyland, and they had always held the fascination of the unattainable. Now, here we were, about to set foot in mysterious Siam! It appeared as a rich, smiling land, intensively cultivated and criss-crossed by canals. Large water buffalo worked in the fields. A rice crop had just been harvested, and the countryside was golden with stubble and haystacks. We saw no troops and no service vehicles. The drive from the airport took us along straight, tree-lined roads, the canals alongside serving both for irrigation and as waterways, with little tented boats plying busily up and down. Then we passed through a rambling city, with some streets typically eastern and others wide and modern looking.

One broad avenue under construction contained a striking monument with four outstretched wings, which we were told represented the wings of democracy.

There were no English signs. The Thai characters looked not unlike Sinhalese, and the language sounded equally harsh.

Our destination was again the YWCA hostel. Here we were received with consternation! Didn't we know that the country was out of bounds to service personnel on leave? There was sure to be an enquiry, and trouble! Our guilty hearts sank, and in those first moments our thoughts flew to possible means of escape - but not before we had seen something of our coveted goal! The woman in charge of this YWCA hostel was a charming Australian - clearly friendly as well as competent - but she was worried. She explained that she was obliged to report all arrivals to the Army, but she promised to do her best to smooth things over.

We rang up Tony - our medical officer friend. He came at once, surprised to see us, since, when the ban on Thailand was announced, he had written advising us not to come - only his letter had not arrived before we left Singapore. Whatever he may have felt, he was immediately reassuring, and he was confident that all would be well. In the meantime we must enjoy ourselves. He then took us off to tea at the naval officers' mess, where we were welcomed with warmth and some amusement. There was much speculation as to what the Army could do about us anyway. It was perhaps just as well that the Naval-Officer-in-Charge was away at the time; our arrival might have been an embarrassment to him!

That evening Tony was booked for a party with some of the Thai royal family. He promised to try and get us included in the invitation - and this he did. We went to the home of a prince and princess - cousins of the King. (King Ananda Mahidol, who was assassinated later that year, and succeeded by this brother, King Bhumibol Adulyadej). Here cocktails were followed by a delicious buffet supper, for which our hostess told us she had cooked some of the dishes herself. The party grew as the evening wore on, with the arrival of more and more royal relatives, as well as a number of British naval officers. The latter seemed to be very popular with the princesses.

The Thai women are petite, and superbly graceful. The girls we met were charming, sophisticated, and beautifully dressed, in European style. I was told that part of their education had been in France. There was nothing to suggest a recent disruption of their way of life, and certainly no sign of post-war shortages.

The Thai greeting (wei) consists of placing the hands with palms together in front of the face and bowing over them in a graceful gesture. I was struck by the beauty and expressiveness of the women's hands - so supple that the fingers bend right over backward, as required for their national dances, taught in childhood.

After dinner we went on to a fashionable club. The decor was striking, and in the centre of the dance floor an enormous fountain played over multicoloured lights. We watched a performance of the Ramwong, a round dance, typically oriental and subtly erotic, in which the partners never touch. We were told that the King had been at that club the previous night. We did not see him during our stay, though our naval friends told us that they were frequently in his party.

* * *

As anticipated, Helen and I were summoned to appear before the senior army officer the following afternoon to explain our presence in forbidden Bangkok. Our only worry was that we might have brought trouble to some of the RAF personnel who had been kind enough to help us.

A surprisingly young colonel received us in his office and did his best to be stern and disapproving, and to impress upon us the enormity of our offence; but his solemnity was short-lived, and soon he invited us to tea. It appeared that he and one captain were the sole occupants of a requisitioned palace, where they were living in great style. After tea, at which a number of servants handed round fruit, sandwiches, and fancy cakes, the colonel asked us if we would like to see over the palace. We passed through a succession of sumptuously furnished apartments and corridors. Then our host paused before a door, which he flung open with a flourish as he declared: 'and this is my bathroom'. His pride was understandable when we looked upon that expanse of tinted marble and gilt-framed mirrors, with, in the centre, a sunken bath large enough to accommodate a fair-sized harem. We were suitably impressed. We felt confident that no very severe measure would be taken against us!

The YWCA, situated in a pleasant bungalow and garden, was run by one Australian and one New Zealander - both women who had seen a good deal of the war and of the world in general. Comforts that one had learned to appreciate: plumbing that worked, spring mattresses, and good fresh food served on fine china, all contributed to our enjoyment. No doubt because of the restrictions on the area, we were the only guests at the time, which gave us an extra degree of freedom. A few days after our arrival, and while we were still 'in funds', Helen and I joined with our hostesses in giving a party, which was a great success and continued into the early hours. Needless to say, our colonel of the sunken bath was among our guests.

On another memorable evening we were entertained at a party afloat. Two barges coupled together provided dining space and a splendid dance floor. As we glided up the river in dazzling moonlight, we were hailed from some ghost-like ships of the Thai navy moored along the bank.

There was much to see in Bangkok. The floating markets on the klongs (canals) were fascinating and carried on a brisk trade. *(Waterway trading was then widespread and not - as now- confined to the main floating market preserved as a tourist attraction. Likewise, many of the klongs have since been filled in and built over as motorways.)* There were boats laden with luscious looking fruits, some of which I have never seen elsewhere, exotic flowers, vegetables and foods of all kinds, as well as household goods, and of course the 'boat people' carried on their daily lives afloat.

The silks and the jewellery in the shops were tempting in the extreme, and our small supply of ticals (the Thai monetary unit before adoption of the Baht) soon melted away.

On our sight-seeing expeditions, and while our naval friends were busy, we travelled by trishaw. This tricycle variation of the rickshaw - which we had first seen in Penang - seated two passengers side by side, with a man pedalling the cycle from behind. One afternoon we were bowling along a quiet road when we saw a herd of water buffalo - presumably just released from work - lumbering along in the charge of a small boy, and obviously making for a klong. We were in their direct path, and for some awful moments it looked as if we must be overturned and trampled by those great cumbersome beasts. However, the herd parted and branched round us just in time, and we watched the animals flop happily into the water and immerse themselves so that only their snouts showed above the surface.

On some of our outings, and even in the garden of the YWCA hostel, we would be embarrassed by the sight of Japanese workmen retreating before us walking backwards and making a deep obeisance every few steps. We were told that this token of subservience was demanded of all surrendered personnel in Thailand.

* * *

All too soon our adventurous leave came to an end. It had come up to all our expectations. We realised how lucky we had been, and we were grateful for much help and kindness. Now it was time for us to return to our posts in Singapore. But here our troubles began! Clearly there had been a tightening up of regulations on travel.

At the RAF Booking Centre we were told that all seats on planes flying into Singapore were being requisitioned for the transport of accused persons and witnesses required to give evidence at the War Crimes Trials. The RAF would be happy to take us as far as Rangoon, but from there we would have to take our chance, and of course we had no claim to priority.

A sign at Bangkok Airport always comes to mind when I am frustrated by delays on air journey: 'Time to spare? Travel by air'. We realised that we were in for a long wait and were determined to be as comfortable as possible. The VIP lounge looked inviting, and it was empty. When we approached the desk clerk and told him that we would be in the VIP lounge when our flight was called, he looked rather dubiously at our unimpressive VAD uniforms, but he said nothing. Later a brigadier came in. He showed no surprise at seeing us there, but there was a twinkle in his eye as we exchanged pleasantries. His flight was soon called, and after he had gone we saw that he had left behind what was unmistakably a lunch packet. I ran after him with it, but was too late, and so, deciding that it was a pity to waste good food, we proceeded to enjoy some delicious chicken sandwiches carefully wrapped in fresh lettuce leaves. We felt sorry for the brigadier, but were sure the RAF would feed him on his way; they always did.

Back in Rangoon - now short of money and frankly worried - we called at the RAF offices at least twice a day. Our leave had expired; my boss was a busy man; and Helen's colleagues were awaiting our return in order to take their leave. During this time our RE friends were tremendously kind and hospitable. One evening, after dinner at their mess, and while we were having coffee on the veranda, we were joined by their CO, whom we hadn't met before. He had been dining out and said he had just heard an extraordinary tale of two nurses who were roaming around the East, regardless of authority, and apparently enjoying themselves hugely. The grapevine had indeed been active. We wondered how this colonel would react, and we sensed some embarrassment among our hosts. "Well, I wish them luck", he said, "I'd like to meet them" - and so he did.

Before we left Bangkok the naval mess had given us a dozen fresh eggs, which were unobtainable in Singapore and very precious. We decided to take them to our colleagues as a peace offering, but as the days went by we feared that we might arrive with a brood of chickens! It was hot by day and cool at night, and so every evening we would place the eggs carefully along the window ledge to discourage hatching.

At last I prevailed upon a civilian passenger with special priority to carry an explanatory - and apologetic - letter to my boss, who pulled strings to such good purpose that seats on a plane to Singapore were made available for us the very next day!

Our luck held. No thunderbolt fell. Our illicit rovings were known only to a discreet and sympathetic few. The eggs were still eggs and were gratefully received.

* * *

On my return from leave I had learned with regret that Captain Rainsford would be departing for the UK very shortly. He was intent on speeding up the machinery of the RN Tropical Research Unit, and there was much to do before he left. I had enjoyed working for him, and I would gladly have stayed on with the Unit - as I was asked to do. However I was due to return to Britain for demobilisation and eventual return to Chile. In the interval I worked mainly for the Medical Division, though sometimes I was detailed to take minutes at meetings of other departments, and it was interesting to see different aspects of the great SEAC machine as it wound down its operations.

* * *

The repatriation of service personnel was being speeded up. Shipping lists were studied eagerly day by day. One after another friends and colleagues were leaving Singapore.

As an alien, I required a re-entry permit from the Home Office before I could return to the United Kingdom. This condition had been impressed upon me before we left Liverpool in 1943, and I knew that the responsibility for having my papers in order rested with me. I had explained all this to a sceptical WRNS drafting officer in plenty of time, but she remained unconvinced; such a thing was not in her 'book of words' and she would have none of it. I was equally adamant; such a regulation could not be ignored. When I appealed to higher authority, steps were taken immediately, but the delay in obtaining the permit caused me to miss my ship. However, I managed to get my heavy luggage aboard the Carthage, where Helen was good enough to take charge of it, accepting my assurance that - somehow - I would be at the other end to see it through customs.

I then set about applying for an air passage. I addressed my request to an Admiral; it worked! RAF planes of all kinds were being converted and used for the transport of personnel, and it was on a York bomber that I returned to Britain in May 1946.

* * *

On the night before my departure - with one of my few remaining friends - I wandered for the last time among those well loved streets, markets and bazaars, ate forbidden Chinese food, and wallowed in nostalgia.

We took off at daybreak, from a strip at Changi, on the north-eastern tip of the island. As the machine was leaving the ground a cow - which had probably been turned loose to graze illicitly on the field over night - ambled across the runway. We must have missed it by inches. We all shared the pilot's reaction, if not his language!

I had one patient, who occupied the seat next to me. He suffered from a septic leg wound which required attention at intervals along the way. A retired judge, who had spent much of his working life in the East, he had fascinating tales to tell, and a delightful sense of humour. Another passenger up in the front was a charming but somewhat enigmatic Scot, apparently a great traveller, and said to have served in the renowned Force 136. And there was an RAF Wing Commander, wearing the traditional handlebar moustache, and also very good company. The rest of the passengers were a cheerful bunch of 'other ranks', all just counting the hours to get home.

By today's standards we travelled at a snail's pace, but in 1946, three-and-a-half days from Singapore to Britain was considered a quick journey.

Our first lap took us north to Pegu, in Burma, for refuelling. We then turned due west, making for Calcutta, where we were hoping to spend the night. As we were approaching Dum Dum Airport, we were overtaken by a dramatic and wholly terrifying tropical storm. The machine was tossed about like a cork in a boiling cauldron. On one side there was a pit of darkness, and on the other blinding lightening. The pilot decided not to attempt a landing. In that part of the world there could not have been many runways long enough to take a York, but eventually - and it seemed miraculously - we were able to get down at an ex-US Air Force base in a place called Chakulia, near Ranchi, about 180 miles west of Calcutta. *(Years later I received an explanation of this providentially long runway from an American who had been stationed at Chakulia. The USAF had used it as a secret base for their B-29 bombers).* The station was officially closed, and frenzied preparations had to be made before we landed - just ahead of the storm. The Americans had left a well-stocked bar, and in it we toasted them gratefully, while their abandoned pin-up girls looked down on us from walls shuddering in the fury of the storm.

The arrival of a woman must have caused some inconvenience at a station where there was no separate accommodation, but soon I was comfortably installed in an adjacent hut. A companionable cow was tethered not far away and, after the storm had passed, it was a peaceful haven. The heat was intense, but some thoughtful and ingenious person had managed to rig up a fan over my camp bed. I was sorry that in the flurry of our early departure next morning I was unable to thank him.

On the second day we crossed India. As a special courtesy to his only woman passenger, our pilot invited me to the flight deck. Sitting in the co-pilot's seat, I spent about an hour marvelling at the intricacies of the machine, and looking down upon a vast, unbroken plain. I was disappointed that our route was too far south of Agra to give us even a distant glimpse of the fabulous Taj Mahal. Flying low and with the wings of the York placed above the fuselage, we got excellent views throughout the journey.

The RAF re-fuelled their passengers as well as their machines at every stop. During flight we were regaled with frequent cups of tea out of thermos flasks, and plenty of substantial sandwiches. These - before the age of plastics - were packed in cardboard boxes. Even if somewhat dry, they were eaten gratefully. A pilot once told me that he disliked carrying passengers who were not well 'ballasted'. Airsickness was not to be encouraged, and indeed, during many flights in small and often bouncy planes, I never knew anyone to be sick while travelling with the RAF.

We spent the second night at a transit camp in Karachi. This was a busy junction, handling the arrival and departure of many flights. The camp was crowded and - not surprisingly - the water supply ran out! With forethought born of experience, I had filled up the little tin tub in my room immediately on arrival, and so had only to skim off a film of suicidal insects when the time came to use it, but many of the transit passengers were left disgustedly high and dry.

Going out to dinner with some of my fellow passengers I was able to see a little of that interesting and rather lovely city - then still part of India. We were fascinated to see many camels being ridden and driven through the streets, where cows and goats also wandered, carefully avoided by fair volume of motorised traffic. In the residential suburbs colourful flowering trees spilled over the wells of secluded gardens, reminding me of the Vina del Mar in Chile. Some of the shops looked tempting, but we had neither time nor money to spend.

On the third day, continuing westward, we skirted the Gulf of Oman, where the water looked like jade, and then the Persian Gulf, where the colour turned to turquoise. Here we overtook and exchanged greetings with a Sunderland flying boat, winging its even slower homeward way.

At midday we put down to re-fuel at Shaibah, near Basra, in Iraq; an inhospitable spot, baking under a merciless sun. The runway scorched ones feet. Cold meat freshly sliced for lunch curled up at the edges as one watched. We were thankful to get up and away, sparing a thought for the men serving there.

On our next lap we got a good view of the Dead Sea, surrounded by extraordinary rock formations, and the huge evaporation pans of the salt industry. The River Jordan looked little more than a muddy stream, and the Suez Canal just a ribbon of silver.

Heliopolis Airport, Cairo, was a vast, buzzing hive of activity, with machines of all kinds landing and taking off. There were great Liberators, Air Masters, and fellow Yorks, many familiar Dakotas, and little Moths and Expediters tucking themselves in between.

Our crew were due to be relieved at Cairo. As they took leave of us, our pilot told us that he was reporting some minor engine trouble, and he thought it unlikely that we would get away that night. Delightedly a party of us made plans to see something of the city, dine at Shepheards Hotel, and then visit the pyramids by moonlight. It sounded just too good to be true - and it was! The repair service must have been highly efficient. We were told not to leave the airport, and soon we were recalled to continue on our way. We had been airborne for perhaps five minutes, and had watched the undercarriage being retracted. Then we saw it being lowered again. Uneasy looks were exchanged. Had the repair been rushed through too hastily, and were we about to make a forced landing? I reached for my seat-belt, and my neighbour did likewise. But our anxiety was short-lived. The pilot came over to explain: Ground Control at Heliopolis had radioed that the wheel of a York had been found on the runway from which we had taken off, and he had to inspect the undercarriage. We would be glad to know that it was intact. We were!

We flew through the third night - sleepless in our upright seats and by this time frankly tired. In the early hours we put down at a base in Tripoli, on the North African coast, which had been used by the Italians and still bore the name Castel Benito. At this, our last stop, we were given a strange breakfast of fish, eggs, and beer! Even my good digestion threatened to rebel.

Soon the blue Mediterranean lay behind us. We crossed the coast at Marseilles, and looked down on the lovely, green countryside of Provence. Not much longer now, and our York sped on like a homing pigeon.

I made my way to the back of the plane and, in the tiny toilet space, changed into 'blues'. How strange and stuffy they felt: the collar and black tie, stockings and stout shoes, the shabby uniform - its City of London brass buttons polished up for just this occasion - and finally a rather battered peak cap.

It was mid afternoon when we touched down at RAF Lyneham, Wiltshire. I stepped out into a thin grey drizzle; a chill wind struck through my unaccustomed stockings. A wave of depression threatened to engulf me, and I felt drawn back to the familiar York. But there was no going back! I followed my fellow travellers into the post-war world.

* * *

I found a bed and a welcome at the Latin American Volunteers House. There, to be sure, were some familiar faces and voices, warmth, and laughter that it was good to hear.

The following day I dutifully reported at Haslar. Miss Waistell had retired, and everyone I met was strange. After some searching, my name was found in a large register. Against it was written: 'Left for Ceylon 1943', followed by a later entry, 'Has not returned'.

After a routine medical examination, I was thankful to be released on six weeks leave, which - by dint of determined 'wangling' and string pulling - I later managed to get extended until my departure. At that time I was furnished with a curious travel document: One First Class Railway Warrant form Portsmouth Harbour to Santiago!

In London my old Alien's Identity Card was disinterred, with many restrictions now lifted and I was issued with a ration card.

London, with all its scars and shortages, was nevertheless a brave new world, with the lights on and the sirens silent, and there was much to explore and to enjoy. This I did, often in the company of friends who had shared many experiences, some of whom travelled to London just to join me on these expeditions.

The first post-war Derby was a light-hearted and thoroughly enjoyable occasion, though - alas - I failed to back *Airborne!*

At Kew Gardens it seemed a miracle that so much beauty could have survived, and it was delicious to linger nostalgically in the warmth of a tropical palm house.

Rain did little to diminish the splendour of the Victory Parade on June 8th. I was unable to see much of the human part - the crowds were too dense - but I got a sight of some of the armoured columns, looking terribly impressive with their mighty and mysterious war machines. As an onlooker one was aware of pride and thankfulness for what had been achieved, coupled with the fervent hope that they might never be needed again.

I studied the shipping lists, and when the Carthage docked at Southampton, I was there to meet Helen and relieve her of my luggage. I had travelled down in uniform, and was able to join the stream of disembarking service personnel, I had some qualms in the customs shed as I watched the entire contents of the luggage belonging to a woman officer ahead of me being turned out, examined, and left for her to re-pack as best she could. However, my Red Cross uniform stood me in good stead. 'That's all right, Nurse' - and with a pat on my shoulder, a smiling official waved me through. In truth I had few possessions of substance at this stage of my wanderings on service pay, though I had managed to stow away a fair number of bottles and a few other 'goodies', so that I need not visit ration-weary friends quite empty handed. I had received invitations from several of my Ceylon colleagues to stay at their homes when I got back to England. The welcome I received on these visits strengthened my resolve to come back and to settle in Britain some day.

Meanwhile I kept in touch with the Repatriation Office in London. This was a hive of activity, dealing with the mammoth task of getting people home. Ships were scarce, and there were frequent changes in dates of sailing and ports of embarkation. I marvelled at the efficiency and the goodwill of those repatriation officers.

* * *

The Tamoroa sailed from Tilbury on July 28th, bound for Buenos Aires, and crowded to capacity with home-bound Latin American volunteers from several countries. There were few people I knew and only a handful from Chile among her passengers, but I was lucky to be able to share a cabin with a kindred spirit - Margaret - whose family I had known earlier in Concepcion, and who had been serving in the WRNS.

The authorities were responsible for getting passengers to their right destination, but, once aboard there emerged problems inevitable to such homeward journeys, and this voyage of the Tamaroa was no exception. Service personnel were not officially demobilised until they were returned to their own country, but of course many felt that they had had enough of obeying orders. Our Captain was not a naturally genial man, and he was at times in conflict with some of his passengers. It was indeed hard - though no doubt inevitable - that ships' captains who had endured and survived untold hardships and perils throughout the war should at the end be burdened with social problems.

Many young families were facing the inevitable problems of reunion: men anxious and determined to take their place as head of their family; children resentful of the authority of - to them - a perfect stranger, and jealous of their mother's attention.

And there were the war brides, parted from family and friends, preparing to face life in a strange continent, learn a strange language, and meet unknown 'in-laws'. Unhappily there was not enough cabin accommodation for all the married couples, and in many cases married partners were separated. On the crowded decks there was little chance of privacy.

Despite the strains and tensions, the long voyage did to some extent provide a settling period. Family relationships began to fall into place. As families got to know each other, there was a chance to exchange views and to take stock. Most returning service personnel had fears of one kind or another - not least of how they could fit again into a way of life from which they had been so far removed.

In due course we came full circle, back into the turbid waters of the River Plate.

There we saw again the hulk of the German battleship Graf Spee, much smaller now, as she had settled into the river bed.

We were packed and ready to disembark as we came within sight of Buenos Aires, and we made out a cluster of people waiting on the quayside. Suddenly a violent jolt threw many on their faces. The ship lurched wildly, then steadied, and settled at an angle of about 30 degrees. The Tamoroa had run aground!

All the tugs in the port of Buenos Aires failed to dislodge her at high tide. More tugs were brought in from Montevideo the next day, and fresh attempts were made after the remaining fuel was pumped out - but to no avail. Boats of all kinds flocked around, but no one was allowed to leave the ship; and there we stayed for two days, before being taken ashore in lighters. The crowd on the quayside had dwindled, but the people that remained - cold and tired as they must have been - were warm in their welcome.

I spent a few days with relatives in Buenos Aires, before crossing the Andes once more - and so back to my family and home in Santiago. It was evening when I arrived, and together we stood and watched the glory of the sunset colouring the snow-capped mountain peaks - changeless and reassuring in their majesty.

Hove, Sussex,

1987

APPENDIX

The sinking of the Andalucia Star on 6.10.42.

Extract from a letter to her family in Chile, published in The South Pacific Mail, and kindly made available by Joan Cooper.

"I never dreamed that I would be writing this letter as a ship-wrecked volunteer, but so it is. We were having a wonderful time on the Andalucia Star and thinking how lucky we were to be on a comfortable liner instead of on a crowded ship bringing the other group that left Buenos Aires the same night. We were five girls from Chile; most of the passengers were from Argentina.

The Andalucia Star was equipped with cold storage as a regular meat carrier and she left Buenos Aires with a full cargo. We passengers were travelling in luxury: two of us sharing a stateroom, with a stewardess to look after us, and the meals were excellent. We did have some duties: lessons in Morse code were given and there was quite strenuous PT every day. Games and competitions were organised, and on October 6th the volunteers put on a concert.

That was the night it happened - just after we had sung "God Save the King". At ten minutes to ten there was a tremendous crash and the ship shuddered from the impact of two torpedoes on the starboard side, one of which wrecked the engine-room.

We had our lifejackets with us (as at all times) and we ducked our heads into them as we rushed up to the top deck. However many of us had left our emergency bags in our cabins, because they were too heavy to carry around all the time. Now it was too risky to go down for them, though some of the married men did go down to collect things for their wives. We were wearing only very light clothing, but it was warm, and we always carried our passports and any valuables in water-tight belts.

The crew were wonderfully organised and an officer took command of each boat. Mine was Boat 5, which was lowered very slowly, so that we were still suspended in mid air when the third torpedo struck on the port side, narrowly missing one of the boats already in the water. Then the ship began to sink quite rapidly.

Boat 2, carrying mostly women and the two child passengers, was badly handled and capsized just before reaching the water. One infant, too small to wear a lifejacket, slipped from the arms of her mother, who just managed to grasp her by the hair as she went under. The other little girl, aged 5, drifted away for about half a mile before being picked up, still clutching her doll.

Our stewardess, the bar-tender, and a male passenger who refused to get into a boat were lost. It was feared that the captain had gone down with the ship, as he was last seen on the bridge, but he had managed to escape on a raft, together with the ship's carpenter, the latter unfortunately so badly injured that he died soon afterwards. Several people had narrow escapes and were only located by the lights on their lifejackets.

There were 44 of us in Boat 5, and everybody not rowing was ordered to keep down in the bottom. I've never been so near to suffocation, with my head under the seat and a fat engineer sitting on my back! However, I managed to get my head out in time to see the Andalucia Star as she sank, soundlessly and upright to the end, just 35 minutes after the first torpedo struck. The crew members in our boat were greatly moved: "There she goes, as grand as ever", and "Sinking like a lady", were some of their remarks.

No one saw the submarine, but it was appreciated that although searchlights were played on the sinking ship, there was no machine-gunning of the lifeboats in the vicinity, and the timing of the third torpedo had certainly enabled everyone to get off the ship. *

I don't think anyone slept that first night. There was much signalling regarding the whereabouts of people who were separated from their relatives. In the early morning we had some chewing gum and we tidied ourselves up as much as possible. Sanitary arrangements were set up in the stern, screened by a sail. During the day we were issued with rations of pemmican, chocolate, biscuits and Horlicks tablets. Nearly everyone was seasick; not only those who had been in the water. But spirits were good, even when we went through a belt of heavy rain and everything got drenched. Three of the life-boats converged and were lashed together. It was estimated that we were about 200 miles from land, and we made for it, hoping that a destroyer might come in response to SOS signals.

About 4 o'clock on the second morning we were rescued by a Royal Navy corvette - the Petunia. She had been out hunting U-boats, and had nearly mistaken our lifeboat for one! The remaining lifeboats were also rescued, and relatives were reunited. The Petunia got us into Freetown at about 8 o'clock that evening. There we were transferred to a Free French liner, the President Doumergue, as a temporary measure. In the morning we were taken ashore, where the small British community generously provided us with the most necessary clothing out of their depleted stores, as they had been helping shipwreck victims for a long time. While we were in the harbour we saw the Esperance Bay come in, and our fellow Latin American volunteers aboard her also sent us some clothing and other necessities.

Some days later we were transferred to a British troopship, on which, travelling in convoy, we completed our journey to the UK without further incident."

* * *

* **Note**:

It was thought that the submarine which torpedoed and sank the Andalucia Star might have been under Italian command.

Some of the survivors who were landed at a Scottish port saw the following item in a local newspaper dated November 1st:-

"Hitler has conferred the Iron Cross on Admiral Grossi for his 'success' 200 miles from Freetown on 6th October."

Eileen Ramsey nee Wright

From March 1944, I had been at the Red Cross Auxiliary Hospital at Sandon Hall, Stafford nursing women and children evacuated from Birmingham hospitals. The hospital was emptied completely just prior to 'D-Day' ready to admit casualties.

Eileen Ramsey

When I was nineteen in September, I applied to go mobile (enter the services). I went to Burton on Trent for my Mother's birthday on 27th November. It was then that the whole town rocked with an explosion in the underground bomb storage depot at Fauld where there was much devastation and so many people killed. I felt that going to Portsmouth with its bombing might be safer than staying at home.

I set off for Portsmouth and arrived at the harbour to find there was no Haslar pinnace (small craft transport) to meet me with my heavy suitcases. Some matelots (sailors) kindly helped me on to the ferry and across Pneumonia Bridge to reach the hospital. Having seen Miss Waistell, I was sent to N Block for the night to one of the big double bunk dormitories.

The next morning, two other new girls and I went down to breakfast in our outdoor uniforms only to be sent away to put our hats on. I had learnt the first of Haslar's rules, always to have our heads covered. We had our medicals followed by injections, next a trip to the gas chamber at Portsmouth dockyard to test our gas masks and obtain our identity tags, then on to the wards.

I was sent to B5 ward with Sister Legge, a fearsome introduction for a 'greenhorn' for she was an efficient Sister who ruled with a 'rod of iron'.

Coming up to Christmas, I was moved to the Royal Naval Air Station at Eastleigh, after a few days at Ashfordby, the house in Eastleigh where sick personnel were nursed. Then onto the council flats in Swaythling, Southhampton where the WRNS's lived, their quarters on the camp having been bombed. The sick room was in a flat. I felt a bit strange being on my own in a flat. I was only nineteen and this was my first experience of being alone. There had been a lot of problems with intruders, being all girls in these quarters it rather attracted undesirables. We had had drunken men coming up the fire escape and strange men knocking on doors. I kept feeling there was someone outside my window as I was on the ground floor. I got one of the WRN's to come and have a look a couple of times, there was no-one about. Then one night I had been to see a sick friend at the hospital. There were some people outside the flats, a man had been arrested, he was caught having forced open my window and was peeping through the curtains. I never really felt safe there again. I was rather surprised that a guard was not put outside these flats.

I had very little to do at the sick room, I very rarely had a patient. I also used to cycle down to take the WRN's morning surgery with the MO. I stayed until 'up spirits' which was when the SBAs were issued with their tots of rum. They often gave me a little, which was very nice. The rest of the day was my own and I was bored. The dentist was looking for work and whilst there he insisted on taking my fillings out and replacing them. He also warned me that if my wisdom teeth did not appear shortly I should seek further treatment, advice I was to ignore and regret later.

Advice I received from the MO Surg. Lt. Wingfield, who had just been invalided back from the Far East, I would have done better to ignore. He constantly said to me, "Promise me you won't go abroad. Terrible things happen to nice English girls out there". I was too young to realise he might be wrong or come across one odd case so on my return to Haslar I refused Sister Tope's many entreaties to volunteer to go abroad.

The airfield was attached to Cunliffe Owens aircraft factory and the test pilots would be testing the aeroplanes there. The sick bay phone would ring and a voice would say, "There's been a crash on the airfield, will you send an ambulance". Everything would go on 'stand by'. Fortunately the test pilots would be standing there saying, "What's all the fuss about?".

A boy from my home town was on a Landing Craft Tank running from Southampton Harbour across the Channel with supplies. I got to know many of his friends. We used to play cricket on an LCT (Landing Craft Tank) moored in the harbour, the ball often went into the sea. We used long handled fishing nets for fielding the balls out of the water. We used to have a good laugh, it was a relaxing break between our duties. Sometimes we visited the 'Cowherd' pub on Southampton Common, occasionally hitching a lift back. The day before VE day found us dancing on tables there and generally enjoying ourselves. We hitched a lift back to quarters, a car stopped, picked up the four of us, two 'subbies', a PO Wren and me, were our faces red! We all went silent. We had hitched a lift with an Admiral! He proved to be very nice, dropped us in turn at our different quarters. I might tell you we were rather shocked, not because he was nice but because he was an Admiral and anyone knowing the RN would know what I was talking about.

Before the end of May 1945, I was back at Haslar, working on Junior Officer's Medical. I loved being at Haslar with its routine and always busy. I soon learnt Haslar's other rules; must not walk down the Quarter Deck (a terrible crime), always sign in and out, when collecting our mail in D Block we must not open and read it until we reached N Block, not to wear too much lipstick, cap straight on the head, not to wear black 'silk' stockings - the last three only when Madam was having a 'Blitz', lastly, not to talk to SBAs except in the course of duty.

One day, one of the patients asked if I could fetch his laundry from his ship in the dockyard. I was escorted by the dockyard police to the ship, where I picked up his 'laundry' then I was escorted out again. Never could make up my mind whether they were protecting the dockyard or me! Next morning I realised I had smuggled out two bottles of gin, of course the patient might not have known, his mates might have put it in with the laundry, really though I think it had been part of the exercise. Anyway, he had too much to drink and seeing as he was in with a stomach ulcer it wasn't very clever of him.

I went on to night duty, twenty eight nights of twelve hours on and twelve off. I was there on VJ Day, standing outside Officer's medical listening to the Thanksgiving service from St Luke's Chapel. It will always be in my memory, the war had really ended, we could all start building our lives again.

Miss Gillanders, our Matron did rounds one night. We sat in the ward room making swabs and dressings, Nurse Harvey, an SBA and myself. We stood up as she came in, not a word did she say, just eyed us up and down for what seemed like five minutes. I don't know what thoughts were going through her mind, perhaps we were 'all correct' so she had nothing to say! Anyway she floated out again without a word.

On my last morning, I was summoned by Sister to go to a Royal Marine Captain's room. This officer had always been very obliging about being woken up first in the the morning. Opening the door, I got a lathered shaving brush straight in my mouth. His revenge (with Sister's connivance) for all those early calls, which only goes to show all men are boys at heart!

I was moved on to M3 and found I did most of the 'running' since with Haslar's constantly changing staff, I was the only person who knew where the various hospital departments were - laboratory, pharmacy, medical duty cabin etc. I quite enjoyed visiting all the different departments.

A move to the isolation hospital in Portsmouth, where there was a Naval Wing followed. On my first evening we dined with the nursing staff. We were allocated places 'below the salt' (bottom of the table). I sat with Connie Lane who had just returned from South Africa, she was used to insects and insects we had! Ants .... at the dining table! I took advice from Connie and flicked them off the plate, 'uggh', as they crawled all over the table, thought I would not like living in this place. A visit while on night duty to collect my handbag which I had left on a shelf under the table, was quite a shock. I was half way across the room when I discovered I was running across a 'sea of beetles'. The whole floor appeared to be moving. It was one mass of beetles. I grabbed my bag and beat a hasty retreat. I was to spend five weeks on night duty there, the last part of it on my own with twenty four patients to barrier nurse which meant putting on a gown etc. each time you entered their room. There was mumps, measles, chicken pox, meningitis, scarlet fever to name a few. We had a walk way where the gowns were hung and the hand basins were placed. Each cubicle had its own gown. An impossible task first thing in the morning to take temperatures, wash patients and make beds single handed before the day staff came on, washing hands and changing gowns before each individual 'operation'.

I was a patient myself next, severe toothache had me back at Haslar, those wisdom teeth. They were impacted and had to be removed. The dentist had warned me!

After a short stay working in the operating theatre, I was put on F5. It was there that the routine of a Haslar ward was imprinted most forcibly on my mind. Pulling out the beds first thing every morning to spread wet tea leaves on the polished 'deck' before sweeping. This took up all the fluff from under the beds. Then 'bumping' the floors with the big polishers. Fortunately, there were often up-patients who liked to help with this. We then cleared locker tops and tidied up for 'rounds'. Then, of course, there were the big double coal stoves in the middle of the wards with all their smoke and dirt. For some reason, F5 had endless patients on treatment during the day. I never discovered where some of the up-patients slept, I know we were kept very busy. We had "Offenders" (prisoners) brought in with Naval Police escort clumping down the ward. Men who swallowed needles, these were given cotton wool sandwiches, they ate anything, buttons, even broken cutlery because they preferred hospital to the Glasshouse (service prison). A guard was by their bed all the time and their

N Block - RNH Haslar, May 1946
Back: **Yvonne Knight, Maureen, Eileen Wright** *Mid 1:* **-, -, Betty Adkins, -, Erica Knight, -, Judy, Monica** *Mid 2:* **Madge Grubb, Kitty Reid, Jean Workman, Miss Waistell, 'Liddy' Lidguard, 'Windy', Savigna Togni.** *Front:* **Ann, Mary Schofield, 'Hether', -, Barbara**

discipline was very strict. I spent Christmas on F5, putting up decorations for the short time allowed. The Surgeons served the midday meal. We stayed on duty on Christmas Day. There was a concert in the D Block mess in the evening.

There was a wonderful companionship on N block in 1945-46 when Miss Workman was there with Liddy and Heather. It was really the old mental block. We did our ironing in the padded cell, had hot lemon drinks or ships 'Kai' (which was a gooey chocolate drink) at night. We stood on a mound in the garden to look over the sea wall, went swimming off the sea wall in the summer or walked along there for some fresh air. We got a fright one day while walking along, three strange shapes came out of the sea, were they aliens or creatures of the sea? It was something we had never seen before - frogmen - when they took their masks off we realised they were men. Maybe they had been seen before, but not by us. It had all been very 'hush hush' during the war. New inventions were kept under wraps and seeing these objects coming out of the water at night was rather heart stopping. Today, they are an everyday occurrence, but this was a first sight.

An invitation came for three well-behaved, well-brought up young ladies of 20 or under to go to a party on HMS Frobisher. There being only two of us in hospital of that age, Joyce Carnaby looked only this age so she was ordered with us by Madam to go, with instructions to wear our knickers with elastic legs so that the men in the boat below would not be able to see anything as we went up the side of the ship. The three of us had a good laugh about this, we also wondered who had written the invitation in the first place! Anyway, we enjoyed the party, the ship had just come back from the West Indies and had fruit on board we had not seen since children. We ate endless bananas and indulged in all the 'goodies'. We were really pleased we had been 'detailed' to attend.

Another highlight, the only social function held at Haslar, was the SBAs' dances in Ertoll Hall. They were great fun and very friendly. I don't remember if we danced to a small band or records but typical forties music. There would be about 150 people there.

In November 1946, expecting demob, I had been on an educational Vocational Training Course to Mill Meece in Staffordshire and having been told that everyone had weekend leave at the end I went home. On arrival back at Haslar, I was told that weekend leave applied to everyone but VADs and I had to write a letter of apology to the Admiral dictated by Madam, finishing 'I remain sir, your most humble and obedient servant'. I felt that my move early in the New Year 1947 was punishment for blotting my Haslar copybook. Three or four of us were sent to the WRNS Training Camp at Burghfield, a virtually all-female establishment with little access to transport into Reading. It was a 'strange' place. The Medical Officer ordered all incoming VADs to spend their free time in the sitting room set aside for us in the sick bay. The bad weather of 1947 (thick snow) started shortly after our arrival and the sick bay being the only warm place on the camp we were invaded by field mice. They ran up and down the curtains, were in the upholstered chairs, ran across our beds, were in the cornflakes, were everywhere. On night duty again, I came back after answering a patient's bell to find four of them on my plate eating my supper! Hamlin Town with their rats had nothing on our field mice. The Duty Wren was supposed to bring the ship's cat to the sick bay last thing at night but even if she could catch it, for it was half wild, it was not interested. Cats hunt for sport and enough is enough. It would have needed to hunt 24 hours a day to keep that lot down! It was April before all the snow disappeared and the mice left us.

I was demobbed there in July 1947. I had enjoyed my life as a VAD in the Royal Navy. It was an experience I would not have missed.

N Block - RNH Haslar, May 1946
Back row left to right: **Moyra Salmon, Joyce (Me) Cornaby, McIlwraith, Walters,-**
Second row from back: **Valerie Doe, Marjorie Harrison** *(both in outdoor uniform)*
Third from back: **Miss Workman, Madam Miss Waistell** *(middle)*, **Yvonne Knight** *(end)*.

Kindly supplied by Mrs. Joyce Pearson nee Cornaby.

HMS Jackdaw, Crail and RNH Kingseat

These are the Scottish hospitals which were in great use during the war.

Joyce Drury

Extracts from "The Weekend Scotsman" newspaper of Saturday, January 11, 1986

The Service men and women who were stationed at HMS Jackdaw, the Royal Naval Air Station at Crail, remember the posting as among the "best days of their lives". Off duty the men struck up lasting relationships with local girls in the Snakepit, the station's own dance hall.

Between the snakepit and jackdaw's nest.

Edward and Norman Dixon recall life in the now-derelict base.

The small town of Crail in the East Neuk of Fife has been invaded twice this century, once in 1917 and again in 1939. Fortunately these were friendly invasions. The first occurred when the young men and women of the Royal Flying Corps came to 27 Training Depot Station on Fife Ness to become pilots and auxiliary staff.

In 1918 these British trainees were joined by the first American airmen to come to Scotland, learning to fly the Avros and Sopwiths so desperately needed on the Western Front. The stay at Crail for both Yanks and British was short however, the station being closed in March 1919 when the grass runways reverted to farmland.

Despite its brief lifespan there was time enough for two fatal accidents to occur. Miss Janet Watson of Anstruther, who was a member of the Women's Auxiliary Air Force at Crail, clearly recalls how one pilot smashed into the sergeants' mess and another narrowly missed the women's living quarters. Buried in St Mary's Churchyard, Crail, the fliers' graves were the first of many which were to follow in the Second World War.

After 20 years of agricultural tranquillity, this ideal site once again attracted the attention of the Ministry of Defence. This time the task was to be more specialised , the training of qualified pilots in the new technique of launching torpedoes from aircraft. The operation was on an unprecedented scale.

Overlooked by Balcomie House, traditionally a home of Mary of Guise, the mother of Mary Queen of Scots, men and machines laboured laying permanent runways and creating a massive complex of workshops, living quarters, a purpose-built cinema and dance hall, fondly remembered as the "Snakepit", and a chapel, all dominated by the stark outline of the control tower. The Royal Naval Air Station, HMS Jackdaw, was born, named as are all such establishments after creatures of the air.

The particular creatures inhabiting this jackdaw's nest were at first Walruses and Swordfish. The latter, affectionately known as the "stringbag", predominated until summer 1942 when it was joined in turn by Albacores, Stukas, Bothas, Beauforts, Rocs and finally Barracudas.

Occasional visitors from nearby Leuchars were Handley Page Hampdens, known as "potato mashers" and "flying suitcases" due to their profile and as "sardine tins" because of the cramped accommodation and poor escape facilities. Hampden crews trained at Jackdaw helped to sink the German Battleship Tirpitz in Tromso Fiord in Norway in November 1944.

Their expertise in torpedo dropping was gained on the range off May Island where the technique was to approach the target ship from a considerable height, dive steeply, and then release the practice dummy torpedo while skimming just above the waves.

It was at this point most accidents occurred, caused by the instability induced on the sudden release of the torpedo or by being too close to the water. Twenty-one of the twenty-two white headstones of the Commonwealth War Graves commission in St Mary's Churchyard are evidence of the tragic price paid by those young trainees far from the battlefront. . . . .

Thankfully not all of the incidents were tragic. Mr Thomas Richardson, a native of Crail and in charge of the transport workshops at Jackdaw from 1939 until 1947, remembers a Lockheed Hudson which had been badly shot up over Norway being forced to use Jackdaw for any emergency landings. ......the pilot brought his plane down intact, though missing the runway.

Unfortunately for the flier, so house-proud were they at Jackdaw, that, far from getting well-earned praise, he received a severe reprimand for damaging the turf!

Bruce Milne of Dollar, a Fleet Air Arm fitter, confirms that everything about Jackdaw and not just the grass was "tiddly". Helping to keep personnel as "tiddly" as the station, were the entrepreneurial ratings of the "dhobi" firms, who, for a fee approved by the station commander, did the laundry for all ranks. In this, as with most other aspects of everyday life, Jackdaw was virtually self-sufficient though local shops received extra supplies to cater for the few Jackdaw men and women who were "victualled ashore".

It was in the areas of entertainment and personal relationships that the impact of Jackdaw was most felt locally. With the camp personnel outnumbering the 1,500 local inhabitants by almost two to one, it was inevitable that lasting relationships would be formed. Marriages between local girls and servicemen usually involved permanent staff as training courses lasted only ten weeks.

Many romances also blossomed on the station as might be expected with so many healthy young adults thrown together far from home. For these young folk the epicentre of romantic life on Jackdaw was the "Snakepit". Although many navy men and women would go on "liberty" as far as Dundee and the cinemas and dance halls of East Fife boomed, it was to the "Snakepit" that both service personnel and local civilians went to dance to the latest hits from America and Britain played by their own dance band. . . . .

In addition to being a dance hall the "Snakepit" was also the camp cinema where three prime seats were reserved for off-duty nurses from the station hospital situated a quarter of a mile from the camp in the former Forelands Hotel, Marketgate. One of the nurses who often occupied one of these seats was Miss Annie Flowerday. In a lifetime of nursing she spent her first three years at the navy hospital and was thus in a unique position to observe wartime life both in Crail and in camp.

Food for service personnel at the hospital and at Jackdaw was certainly superior to that enjoyed by most civilians. Convalescing patients collected seafood for the hospital from the harbour at Crail. One patient even became expert in dressing lobsters though Miss Flowerday disliked them describing them as "running round the galley like great big black forkie tails"........

Christmas dinner at Jackdaw in 1943 included roast leg of pork, ... when such luxuries were but fading memories to civilians.

Almost as essential to the wartime Navy were their issues of tobacco and rum. The tobacco was the much-loved Tickler brand in its distinctive red and green tins selling at 2/6d (12 1/2p) per pound. The red tin was for roll-ups and the green tin for pipes.

Some of this tobacco found its way into civilian hands, just one of the ways in which life at the station impinged on that of the locals. So used did they become to the proximity of this large establishment that they came to accept even such curious sight as planes being taxied, wings folded, for dispersal at dusk right in the middle of Crail. . . . . .

. . . . . the buildings have now fallen into a state of disrepair. On encountering a recent visitor to the town returning to his former haunts, Tom Richardson apologised for the present state of the officers' mess explaining that it was now full of pigs.

"It always was", replied the former Jackdaw man.

Many men and women remember their Service days as "the best days of our lives", a time when it was glorious to be young and free of those domestic responsibilities which later years bring. To those who served at Crail, Jackdaw was part of this.

Extracts reproduced with kind permission from the Weekend Scotsman 08/11/95

Extract from a Commemorative Booklet about Kingseat Hospital

Little is accessible in the way of records about Kingseat during the years, but many readers will know that the Navy left its mark. The most dramatically nautical evidence today, nearly 50 years later, is on the back wall of the stage in what was built as the Recreational Hall and has been used, temporarily (!) as the Industrial Therapy Department since late 1967. The wall is painted as the fore deck of a battleship, complete with huge grey gun turret.

Perhaps more useful were other legacies in the form of buildings, some still in use.

Craigie Villa, the Nissan hut in the field beyond Maudsley, in use till 1974, was built as the NAAFI Canteen. The old Social Club Room now used as a domestic staff headquarters and store and formerly the staff dining room was built by the Navy as a Kit bag store for patients. The adjacent building houses the Pharmacy. The Navy built the X-ray Department and their surgical unit formally male and female Morel and now the Psychogeriatric Unit was served by a suite containing two operating theatres, last used as such in the early 1950's, converted to use as our first Industrial Therapy Department in about 1961 and now upgraded since 1968 as the Psychogeriatric Day Hospital.

The duty room in Conolly Villa was the Officers' Mess Bar, and the wall there was painted as a desert island with waving palm and a fierce-looking pirate.

It is interesting to note that Kingseat was involved in reverse, so to speak, in the First World War when we took 25 patients from Bangour Hospital in 1915 to free it "for military purposes".

Nurses House, Kingseat Hospital, Aberdeenshire
Photo kindly supplied by Renée Gibb nee Munro

The Scottish hospitals were a very important part of our history and the following four chapters are by our Scottish VADs, namely:

Renée Gibb
Mary Innes-Smith
Christina MacIver
and photographs kindly supplied by Anna MacKenzie

The following poem was written by a patient to one of the Scottish VADs:-

To Dimples

Faith dear lady my presumptuous attitude is deploring, but yet you must find it in your tender heart to forgive a poor patient's meditations, and have in your mind the knowledge that they are due to the trials and tribulation caused by the forced inertia of the body, which houses my tempestuous soul.

Your smile may have been one of gentle pity but no-one, nay, not even Venus in all her majestic splendour could have rivalled the becoming curve of your lips and the fascinating allure of those dimpled, rosy cheeks.

Your sparkling eyes, flashing a million reflected rays of light, are like rare gems destined to be coveted because of their exquisite lustre and radiant perfection.

Your dark, wavy hair adorned as by a halo with the white cap of your uniform seems a confirmation of the genteel purity which I, in unison with many more, attribute to a maiden's nature.

Your slight figure may even rival that of Salome in her youthful glory.

And now I can write no more. My limited vocabulary fails in an effort to do you justice. If I have trespassed or transgressed I offer a thousand apologies and will have a thousand misgivings in my heart.

May your future years be full of joy and happiness. With peace I hope that these islands that are Britain will be a haven of blessed tranquillity in which we may all live, love and learn so we may forget the base, bestial horrors of war for ever.

You have unwittingly helped me to pass an interesting period in a very drab and uninteresting evening and for that

Thank you

R E Payne

Renée Gibb nee Munro

Memories of my time at Royal Naval Hospital, Kingseat, Aberdeenshire

The shock of arriving on a first posting to Kingseat was two fold.

One, the naval jargon, two, being allocated one of 50 bunk beds in a dormitory. To boarding school girls this may have been the norm but to some who had never been away from home it was indeed a cultural shock and the first pang of home sickness!

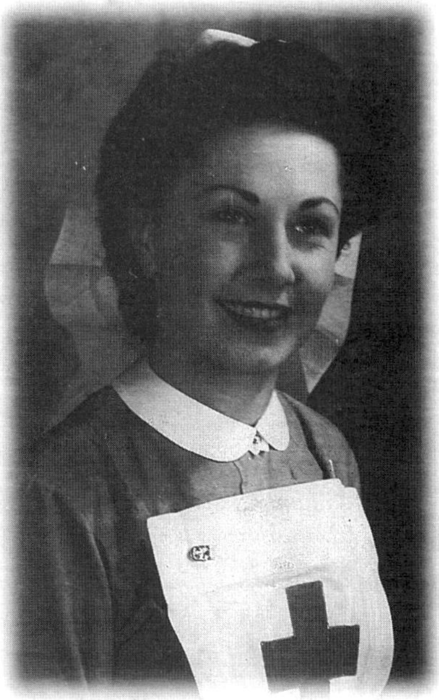

Renée Gibb nee Munro RNVAD
Abbotsinch, Glasgow.

In no time, we were going ashore on the liberty boat, referring to "watches", making tea and toast in the galley and taking ones turn at cleaning the 'heads'. Bumping the polished floors with heavy lead weighted polishers, prior to Captain's rounds, when patients were tucked in 'at attention'. Its a wonder they did not require resuscitation after 'present and correct' was accepted by the top brass.

Kingseat was where we did our initial training, for three months we learned the ways of the Royal Navy and gained our GI badges. Once this was achieved, the next step was a posting to the many naval establishments throughout the United Kingdom and overseas postings.

One foreign draft was mustered to leave Kingseat when the Commandant announced in her strong North country accent, 'The Tirpitz has been sunk'! One wonders what went through the minds of those girls.

The next promotion was to senior VAD which was depicted by a very small strip of red ribbon on the cuff of our walking out uniform. On more than one occasion one was asked in hushed tones if this meant one had been wounded!!

The friendships forged were legion, the laughter and the tears shared was something very special. What better lesson in life could we innocents abroad have learned, than by the respect shown to us on our job, and the compassion we felt for the sailors who, through no fault of their own, were in our hands to be comforted and healed not only from their wounds but also the mental agony many young men suffered.

Kingseat Hospital will always hold its special memories.

RN Hospital Kingseat, Sisters, VADs & patients.

Kingseat Hospital

The fire escape outside nurses quarters,
Left to right: **Bertha, Renée, Eileen,**
Kilmalcohn RN Hospital 1945

Eileen & Renée,
- Kilmalcohn RN Hospital 1945

Abbotsinch 'HMS Sanderling'
Lena Elliott, Renée Gibb.

RNH badge, worn above
the elbow on left arm.

Mary Innes-Smith, RGN (VAD Blue)

Having completed three months at Kingseat, being indoctrinated in Naval ways, on 4th November 1942, I was drafted to RNSQ, Keil, on the lovely Kintyre peninsula, where I was to spend the next three-and-a-half years. The hospital, a large white building, stood in an idyllic spot, on a hillside, overlooking the sea. It was literally "three minutes from the beach, with excellent cuisine", as the brochures might say. The patients and VADs loved it.

Periodically, we were sent out to do short stints at various sick bays in the area. Campbeltown, a busy base, Machrihanish, a FAA station, and Skipness, where there were about a hundred WRNS, known as "bomb markers". Pilots of the FAA did bombing practice in the area.

The solitary VAD at Skipness occupied a hut separate from the WRNS' quarters. It was divided in two by a partition, one half a small sick bay, the other being the VAD's sleeping cabin. One night I was awakened by the sound of heavy breathing and footsteps next door in which there were no patients! I froze with terror, but managed to crawl out of bed and quietly lock the communicating door. Eventually I could stand the suspense no longer and decided to investigate, expecting to find a drunk or a tramp dossing down for the night. So I unlocked the door and flashed my torch, to find half a flock of sheep inside, and the other half trying to get in. The badly fitting door, which didn't lock had burst open in the wind during the night, leaving the hut open to any guests who cared to call. Sheep have a halitosis problem and the pong was atrocious. We stared at each other, then panic set in and they all tried to get out at once.

There was no more sleep for me that night. Who said that counting sheep was no cure for insomnia? When I completed my month's duty, I was delighted to return to the comfort and security of dear old Keil.

Christina MacIver (nee Burnside)

Towards the end of the war in Europe, I was stationed at HMS Lochinwar, a mine sweeping base on the Forth. We had a staff of five MOs, one Sister, four Senior VADs and a few SBAs. As you can imagine, it was a busy Base, but one day stands out above all others . . .

It began at 1 am when another VAD and I were called out with the duty MO to rescue three ratings and two Wrens who had been involved in an accident. We rendered first aid and got them back to the Sick Bay, where they were treated in the small operating theatre and admitted to the wards. We got to bed about 4 am, but had to be on duty again at 5 am to prepare for a visit from the Duchess of Kent (the late Princess Marina). It was a case of all hands on deck, but by 2 pm, all treatments had been completed, the wards looked spotless, the flowers beautifully arranged and all the patients 'lying to attention' in their beds! Outside, the Wrens were drawn up in orderly ranks, but a few were beginning to wilt after standing almost an hour. Contrary to orders, we sneaked out to rescue them, revived them with some tea and managed to get them back in place as the Duchess was beginning her inspection. Afterwards, the Duchess toured the wards, spoke to all the patients, shook hands with the nursing staff and congratulated us on a lovely Sick Bay.

That wasn't the end of the day. A few weeks previously, we had been invited by the Wrens to a belated Easter dance. The invitation stated - "Civilian clothes if possible. Easter bonnets must be worn". Sister, another nurse and I were off duty so we set forth in our pre-war finery and home-made hat! Toward the end of the dance, Tommy Morgan (a Scottish comedian) judged the Easter bonnets. He had quite a difficult task. He awarded a prize for the most original hat. "To the lady who had Princes St. Gardens on her head", (that was Sister). Before presenting the next prize, he remarked that the Navy had obviously gone to the lady's head!, (it was my fellow VAD - in a hat of green net with a toy ship perched precariously on top and sporting the Union Jack!). The prize for the prettiest hat went to "a lady obviously bound for Ascot", (me! - with a frothy concoction of pink tulle, cut from an old dress, and trimmed with two artificial pink roses). To round off the Sick Bay's success, our ambulance driver was voted the most handsome man! Of course, our fame, not only spread round the Base, but reached the ears of the Captain and crew of a mine sweeper in the Forth. As a result, we were invited to take tea with the Captain and enjoyed a sail on his ship. It is wonderful what a little publicity and a hat can do!!

Anna MacKenzie nee MacKay

Anna MacKenzie nee MacKay,
Glasgow detachment, RNVAD Sydney.

RNVADs VJ parade, Brisbane.

Hospital - Ekibin, Brisbane.

Funeral of Matron Westaway, Hong Kong, RNVADs.

Joan Lorenzen nee Morris-Davies W/586251

Joan Lorenzen nee Morris-Davies was one of our army VADs and was in the first batch of VADs to be sent to France after D-Day to join a tented base hospital in Bayeux. She was a VAD from 1939 to 1946 and ended her service time in India.

Joyce Drury

Being Called Up In September 1939

After leaving school I decided to be ready to do something useful in case of war being declared - it seemed inevitable to people of my age group. I became a member of the British Red Cross Society and did a course in Home Nursing and First Aid and felt ready for any emergency! When War was declared, I was told officially to report to the Royal Herbert Military Hospital in Woolwich, and I arrived there on 12th September 1939 complete with all my uniform and my nursing manual. I had been to Garrolds in Tottenham Court Road to buy the necessary blue cotton dresses, aprons, caps, starched cuffs and starched collars and a navy uniform coat and blue hat; we had been told we could claim for the uniform when we reported for duty. Standing beside me, also buying uniform, was an ancient QA Reservist, who looked just like the White Queen in Alice in Wonderland, and had all the assistants rushing around to find all the kit she needed - I hoped very much that we would not meet again!

Joan Morris-Davies holding balloon at Royal Herbert Hospital, Woolwich 1942, with friend Nan. Shows uniform well - note starched collar, and we had starched cuffs to wear when sleeves rolled down and we all had navy capes with red linings.

The Royal Herbert was a large red brick military hospital standing in its own grounds at the bottom of Shooters Hill and it had been built during Victoria's reign. I got there on the back of a friend's motor bike, clutching a suitcase, and reported to the main office to find I was not expected. After much phoning around I was told I would be billeted with a family about one mile from the Hospital, given brief instructions on how to get there and off I went. I was gruffly greeted on arrival by a quaint little man in shirt sleeves and a cap. In all the six months I stayed there I never saw him without his cap, so presumed he slept in it. They also kept chickens permanently in the kitchen where we had our meals. We were supposed to have a two course main meal and breakfast each day, and in all my time there I never had anything but pineapple chunks for pudding! They could be bought very cheaply at the time.

I was told to report to Medical II Ward in the basement of the Hospital and to wait to see the Sister in Charge. Suddenly there was a great commotion and along came the White Queen and her retinue! Just my luck I thought, but she proved to be an excellent teacher and patient with all her raw VADs. Our conditions improved a bit over the months ahead and I was moved to another billet, owned by a lovely couple who had two small children. Now we were able to have our meals in a canteen at the Hospital, so we did not have to be fed. We earned 15/- a week (75p in decimal currency) out of which we had to pay for our laundry, i.e. aprons, dresses, caps and collars and cuffs. We were supposed to wear our caps down to our eyebrows and not wear any make-up; we all became very efficient in making up our caps so that we could quickly pull them down if we saw the Commandant approaching. We also had to remove our lipstick as soon as possible when we saw her coming. The basements of the Royal Herbert had been turned into medical and surgical wards, and a small operating theatre had also been created in the basement. The ground floor was reserved at one end for patients with TB (two wards of forty beds full of them) and the other end for soldiers with infectious diseases and venereal diseases. The top floor housed the Prisoners of War who were sick or injured. We nursed wherever we were sent and had some exciting times during the bombing of the docks and East End of London. There was a direct hit on Woolwich Arsenal at the very beginning of the raids and we all worked for 36 hours with no break except for an occasional meal. I was in the operating theatre at that time and had my eyes opened to the horrors of war.

Night Duty Staff - Summer 1940
Back row: **Hiltermain, Hannay, Wipell, Cedard, Bentley.**
Front row: **Dalziel, Davison, Whitehouse.**
Royal Herbert Hospital, Woolwich.

No. 2 Academy Place, May 1941, This was a house just across the road from the Royal Herbert Hospital in which VADs lived. Joan was in the front ground floor room with bay window when the bomb landed.

VADs In France, Holland and Belgium - 1944/1945

Joan Morris-Davies in Bayeux 1944, showing wash basin! (tin) and cold, wet and muddy boots.

I was with the first batch of VADs to be sent across to France to join a tented base hospital in Bayeux - the 30th BGH. By this time we had been made members of the Forces officially and issued with Army numbers and Army pay books - my number was W/586251 - it is a number I will never forget, it had to be produced on many occasions and especially when we collected our pay! We were issued with khaki battle dress top and trousers, brown lace up boots and leather gaiters; the battle dress top and trousers were made of such rough material that we all went round scratching and tickling horribly. We still wore our Red Cross or St. John hats with the battle dress, and eventually persuaded our respective Headquarters to allow us to wear berets. We also had khaki kit bags in which to lug around our uniforms.

We went across to Arromanches and

travelled on Landing Craft in dreadful weather, eventually disembarking at Mulberry Harbour - a magnificent sight and a wonderfully planned operation. It eventually became very wet and muddy and with only one pair of boots to wear our feet never seemed to be warm or dry. We asked for Wellington boots, but they finally caught up with us when we reached Antwerp! We had to try and dry our washing in the damp tents we slept in in Bayeux and I found the best way of doing this was to put my clean shirt under my blanket on the bed and sleep on it. If I had managed to get at all warm during the night the shirt would be partly dry.

When the fighting moved on through France we had few patients , and these were evacuated back to the UK as quickly as possible. In these circumstances, we were able to have more time off, and not a minute was wasted! We hitched to places like Caen and saw the terrible devastation there and in all the area around. Some French cafes were still open and one, called the White Horse Inn, was very popular. It was surrounded by minefields and difficult to get to, but it still had some wine for sale and calvados, and there was always a fiddler or piper to play gay tunes in the evenings. The floor was rough stone, uneven, but we all managed to dance happily to the cheerful music. We had met some RASC boys who had their own jeep, so we always had a lift, and they had managed to swap something with the NAAFI for a case of whisky, so I rapidly changed from TT to a consumer of neat whisky!!

We eventually moved up to a Base Hospital in Antwerp in the back of several large 10 tonners. It took about three days and was a pretty rough journey but we managed to brew up whenever we stopped for a short while. We reached Antwerp at the height of the bombing by "Doodle Bugs" (radio controlled bombs which cut out the engine when the target was reached, the bomb then dropped and exploded). You never knew when they were going to cut out, but if they did you wasted no time in diving under a bed, or getting away from a window. Sadly, one night a cinema full of Allied Forces received a direct hit and about 600 were killed in that raid. Naturally, we were very busy. A short time later I was moved to the 108 British General in Brussels, which had been a purpose-built civilian hospital standing in large grounds. The VADs had accommodation in the actual Hospital and we had to get a pass to be out later than 10.00 pm. A late pass only lasted until midnight, so one's activities were somewhat limited until we found a place on the 8 ft wall that had a large compost heap on the hospital side. After this find there was no problem getting someone to hitch you up from the pavement outside and then drop safely into the compost heap. (We would have been in trouble if caught, but having lived through so much danger, the risk was worth it!).

Having spent over two years at St Hugh's in Oxford, which was the centre for Neurosurgery in the Forces (mainly Army), I was soon posted to the 8th BGH in the centre of Brussels which covered all the neurological cases, surgical and medical, and also had a maxilla-facial unit. I was sorry to leave all my friends, but we were soon up to our eyes in work. Our Unit was on the top floor of the hospital with a balcony, overlooking the tree-lined street, four or five floors below. In the summer, we had to have the doors onto the balcony open to air the wards, and although most of our patients were not able to move from their beds, we did have some who were mobile and waiting to be sent back to England. There were two occasions when I was on duty on my own when a patient got onto the balcony and tried to climb over the edge and jump into the street below. In each case it was a Polish soldier involved, who spoke little English, so it was not easy to reason with them, but eventually I did manage to get them back into the ward.

VE Day was wonderful for us, we all celebrated in the wards and danced round with anyone who could stand! When we were off duty, we went into Brussels and joined in all the celebrations and danced in the streets all night - a wonderful, ever to be remembered occasion.

All the VADs were asked, I believe in June, if anyone would volunteer to go to the Far East to help with the casualties there and to nurse the repatriated Prisoners of War as they were released. I volunteered with two friends and we were sent back to England and given a week's leave before being interviewed and passed once again as non-army VADs. We then collected bedrolls and more uniform and waited until there was a trooper bound for Bombay available. We finally went on the SS Corfu, full of troops and forty of us. So that was the end of serving in France, Belgium and Holland and we were off to enjoy the heat and sights of the Far East.

A VAD in India - 1945/1946

The journey to Bombay on board the SS Corfu took seventeen days and we were able to go through the Suez Canal. It was not the height of comfort for us as a saloon had been stripped of all furniture, carpets, etc. and two tier bunks screwed to the floor with just enough room between them for us to walk. At one end of the room there were metal cupboards for us to use as wardrobes, but that was the only privacy we had. A communal washroom had been fitted leading out of the cabin, and I believe there were about two showers we could use; the queue for these was always long, no matter what time of day it was.

To get any room on deck was quite a feat and eventually four of us devised a scheme whereby one of the group got up about 5.30 am and went on deck with a blanket, put it down by the rails and sat on it until the others came up after breakfast, usually carrying a cup of lukewarm tea and a bit of bread and margarine for the 'Guard'. After this delicious meal we all got cracking on playing cards, usually bridge, and remained there for the rest of the day. In the evenings a dance was sometimes arranged or a game of Bingo, and very occasionally we had a film show. It got hotter and hotter and we had no tropical kit so had to wear our shirts, navy skirts and black stockings each evening. In the daytime we could wear our blue cotton dresses. It was quite a feat to get our clothes washed, dried and ironed, most of the drying being done by tying things to the sides of the metal bunks.

On arrival at Bombay, we had to dress in our uniform navy suits and march, literally dripping, to the station to catch a train to Poona, where there was a base hospital. Two of the wards had been abandoned by patients to make room for us. As we were only in transit, we had no duties, so were able to go out and buy cotton material to get a couple of thin dresses made - this was wonderful after years of wearing uniform and having practically no clothing coupons. I was to be sent to Singapore and had nearly six weeks of doing nothing but enjoy myself whilst waiting for transport. In the end it was decided to send me and my two friends up to Peshawar on the North West Frontier.

First we were to catch a train to Lahore, which took over 48 hours to reach there, spend a night there and then another train to Peshawar. We went to the station and found a compartment with bunks had been reserved for us, it also had a small space off it with a loo and washbasin. We were a bit surprised when the Guard came along and locked us into the compartment, but as soon as the train started Indians rushed up to it and climbed on to it, hanging onto door handles, windows, etc. and peering in at us. We could not even have a window open, or they would have been in the carriage and we would have been outside! This was their way of getting a free ride. We were very glad when we reached Lahore and then Peshawar. Here there was a General Hospital coping with all the troops serving on the North West Frontier and we were housed in a Mess with only two to a room and one's own bath, albeit tin and having to be filled by a bearer. By now it was December and we had to get navy battle dress made to wear when we were on night duty as it was so cold! One of the things that amazed us most was the complete lack of knowledge the ladies in the Garrison had about what had been going on in Europe. These were the service wives who had spent the hostilities at the Garrison. They had suffered no rationing of food or clothing and knew very little about the War itself. On the whole we nursed the usual everyday medical and surgical cases, but we did still have some cases of typhoid and cholera to nurse as well. There were plenty of activities for us to enjoy when we were off duty and the food was excellent after all the years of rationing.

Eventually in April 1946, we were all to be discharged and sent back to England. By this time I was engaged and so was married and resigned from the VADs, after six years and seven months - a lifetime, but I was proud to have been a member of a very caring and vital service.

Beatrice French nee Stobbs

Beatrice French nee Stobbs served at Haslar during the D-Day landings and she was then drafted to Australia to RNH Herne Bay, Sydney and whilst there she served on HMS Glory, an aircraft carrier which was converted into a hospital ship to take very sick Japanese prisoners of war to Canada.

Joyce Drury

Memories of Haslar, of D-Day and the Normandy Landings

Beatrice French nee Stobbs, RN Hospital, Sydney, July 1945.

I arrived at Portsmouth Harbour Station in the late afternoon of 6th June 1945, a RNVAD en-route for the Royal Naval Hospital, Haslar, to find the transport that should have met me had not arrived and the place agog with talk of the invasion of the coast of France, which had taken place in the early hours of the morning. It had come as a complete surprise, although it had been known that all the country lanes and roads leading to the coast had been building up with armoured vehicles, tanks and men etc. for some weeks past. The people knew something was planned but no-one knew what, until that morning when the news broke. I was young and very pleased I had arrived in time to play my part in it all and to be of some use. I remember looking across the water towards Haslar and seeing dozens and dozens of submarines side by side and nose to tail, stretching across the water like a vast carpet. It was an amazing sight indeed. My transport still had not arrived so I rang the Red Cross Commandant at Haslar to find out what the position was and was informed that they had completely forgotten about my arrival and there was no transport available and that I had better get a taxi, which I did.

My arrival at Haslar was met with a very 'luke warm reception'. I was told by the Assistant Commandant that they could have done without my arrival at that moment in time, they were too busy to bother with me and consequently I was left 'cooling my heels' whilst dedicated activity went on around me.

After a day of this, I decided to make another big effort to see the Commandant and get on to a ward to nurse, which is what I was drafted there to do. I felt very frustrated as I had spent the previous nine months at a Ministry of Pensions Hospital, where (for most of my time there), I had nursed on a surgical ward and helped the nursing sister to dress amputated limbs. The Commandant apparently had thought I was a raw recruit with no experience, but when told of my past nursing experience it was no time before Matron had me posted to a ward.

RNH Haslar at that time was classed as a front line hospital. The hospital ships carrying their wounded from France sailed up the Solent to Southampton where the wounded were disembarked and put on a hospital train and taken to various front line hospitals, the last part of the journey by naval or military ambulances. It was quite hectic at Haslar at first but quite soon tailed off as the troops advanced and field hospitals were set up in France. There were certainly not the number of casualties arriving at the hospital as had been expected though some wards were more full than others. The one I was put on at first was only about half full and had a mixture of British and Americans. After a few days, a week at most, the patients were moved further inland to the next line of hospitals so that Haslar was kept free for more front line casualties.

One of the patients on my ward was brought in unconscious (they all arrived covered in mud and grime and generally very dirty and clothes, very often, had to be cut off them) and he had to be fed by a nurse by mouth with a spoon (no drip feeds then) with food pulped down and liquid from a feeding cup. It always amazed me that, although unconscious, he was able to swallow his food and drink without choking. He never opened his eyes or showed any recognition whilst with us. We also cleaned and freshened his mouth with cotton wool wound around an orange stick dipped in glycerine and he always seemed to know when it was being done for him. He eventually left us, still unconscious, for another hospital further inland.

Another man on the same ward was suffering from shell shock and was raving mad most of the time. He had to be taken to the operating theatre and it took quite a number of SBAs to get him on to the trolley to wheel him down there. It was very distressing. Sadly he died on the operating theatre table.

* * *

For the first two weeks after the Normandy Landings no-one from Haslar was allowed to go ashore (leave the hospital grounds) so when off duty we often used to climb up to the boundary wall of the hospital which faced the Solent and look out for the hospital ships passing on their way to Southampton. You then knew that it would not be long before more wounded would arrive and we would be back on duty again. The bell calling nursing and medical staff back on duty as fresh casualties arrived would be rung at all hours of the day or night calling the 'stand-by staff' on to duty.

It was at that time that the first flying bombs (doodle bugs as they came to be known) were sent across the English Channel by the Germans. They looked like a great ball of fire, made quite a noise, and when the engine cut out dropped down causing considerable damage. As soon as the air raid warning went off of their approach, patients had to be taken from the wards and down into the cellars. If the warning sounded during the night, which was mostly the case, off-duty VADs asleep in their dormitories were to go down to the cellars also, except for those whose dormitories were on the ground floor, as there was not enough room in the cellars for everyone. I was one of those and our instructions were to get out of bed, put on our tin helmets and get under the beds until the all clear. Not many of us were keen to do that, so as our dormitory faced the sea, most of us used to just put on our helmets and still in our night clothes, watch from the windows the flying bombs approaching like a great ball of fire across the sea towards us, holding our breath as it passed over head, waiting for the engine to stop and the bomb to crash to the ground. It was always a great relief when it was all over and to find oneself still alive. One of these bombs did in fact land in the grounds whilst I was there.

As the weeks went on and we had fewer casualties coming to Haslar, I was moved to a Senior Officers' ward and whilst there an Admiral was admitted as a patient. The Sister in charge of the ward would not let any VADs nurse or even enter the room of such a high ranking officer and gave instructions that only Sisters were to look after him and answer his bell when he rang. This lasted until one day he rang and rang his bell and no Sister appeared to answer it, so I did. He was quite surprised to find there were VADs on the ward and asked why he had not seen any of us before and when told by me the reason why he soon had that remedied and from then on we were allowed to look after the 'great man' who was a most charming gentleman.

Haslar at that time was very much in the Naval tradition of Nelson's day. The wards were very old fashioned with old brass taps which had to be kept highly polished even during that period, the wooden floors were kept to a very high shine by the SBAs, polished up every morning with a big oblong polisher on the end of a long handle and woe betide any VAD if a patient's bed was found to be made with the anchor, which was woven into the centre of the counterpane, upside down when Matron did her rounds.

The hospital was built around a large square, the centre of which was a well-kept lawn with a path going all the way round the outside, a path going from top to bottom and another from side to side crossing in the middle. This was called the Quarter Deck and only Naval Officers and Sisters were allowed to use the Quarter Deck and use the paths crossing it, everyone else, including VADs had to walk around on the outside paths to get from one side to the other, this had to be done quite frequently as the laboratory was situated on the opposite side to the wards and specimens often had to be taken and brought back from there. It did not matter how urgent it was, these rules had to be obeyed and, of course, no running was permitted. On the Quarter Deck there was also a flagstaff with a Union Jack flying and the ceremony of raising and lowering the flag was carried out each morning and evening.

All ranks had their own messes. Our VAD mess was presided over by a Red Cross Commandant, Miss Waistell, who had been a VAD in the 1914-18 war and an Assistant Commandant. We had our own Red Cross VAD cooks, who were by all accounts the best cooks of all the messes. Certainly we were the envy of them all because in those grim days we were the only mess who had strawberries and cream for our sweet at dinner, not once but two or three times. Where our Commandant got them from, I don't know but get them she did. She was very strict but she did look after her "girls". Although we were responsible for nursing the sick and wounded on the wards, working in the operating theatre, the laboratory, x-ray department and others, Miss Waistell kept a very tight rein on us and we had to be in and in bed by 10.00 pm with a late pass to 10.30 pm once a week if applied for.

Portsmouth, nicknamed Pompeii in those days, was a mass of ruins due to intensive bombing and to visit cousins of mine living in Southsea I used to take the "Liberty Boat" from Haslar from the small pier in front of the hospital and walk across the bomb sites to visit them.

About two months after arriving at Haslar, and the invasion of France had moved inland from the beaches and field hospitals were set up in France, Haslar returned to normal again and was no longer a front line hospital. I found myself posted and on my way to Liverpool and the Western Approaches, the nerve centre of the "Battle of the Atlantic".

RNVAD - HMS Glory - British Pacific Fleet

On 25th May 1945, I sailed down the Clyde on the "Nieu Amsterdam" bound for Australia and RN hospital Herne Bay, Sydney. Whilst serving there, the war in the Far East ended and the priority was the return of our men who had been POWs under the Japs. To this end a number of aircraft carriers were converted into hospital ships and the last one was HMS Glory.

Early in September, I was summoned into the Red Cross Commandant's office and informed that I was being drafted to HMS Glory to take very sick POWs still in Manila to Canada and to be ready to sail as soon as the ship was ready. The number of VADs the hospital could spare for this mission were eight, so the Australian Red Cross was asked to help and ten Australian VADs (who were part-timers) volunteered.

On 29th September 1945, eight Naval VADs, ten Australian VADs, four QARNNs, four extra MOs to the three already on board and six extra SBAs boarded the ship (along with a small fridge containing precious penicillin) and we set sail that night. We were accommodated in the Air Crew's quarters (recently vacated) and all the nursing Sisters and VADs dined in the wardroom.

The hanger had been divided into two parts, the forward part for the fit men we were to take on board, and the aft had been converted into a hospital. It had double tier bunks, lashed together in fours with the heads together and access for the nurses on one side only. The very sick patients were to be put on the top bunks and the more mobile ones on the lower. The aircraft lift was locked halfway for ventilation and the Sister's Duty Cabin, MO Duty Room, dispensary etc. with a patients' wash room was built. A hatch was set up in the hanger at the side of the hospital so that special food could be prepared.

Early on it was found that the ship's laundry could not starch our aprons and caps the way we were used to and the Nursing Sisters opted to discard wearing their uniforms for nursing in the hanger and wear khaki slacks and shirts with a headscarf tied around their head. It was suggested we should do the same but along with our Australian colleagues, we decided to wear our nurses uniforms as we thought they looked nicer and be a morale booster to the patients and so it proved.

We arrived at Manila on 8th October and proceeded to embark 1350 men of whom 148 were sick and put into hospital, another 16 in the Ship's Sick Bay and more sick on camp beds in the Sick Bay lobby. Seeing the sick carried aboard on stretchers and others trying to walk on their pitiful thin legs with bones protruding under the skin of their emaciated bodies and large Beri Beri stomachs was an emotional sight, but we soon got down to the job of getting them settled in and nursing them. This was no mean task climbing up ladders at the side of bunks in the stifling heat of the hanger in the tropics and the heaving and motion of the ship in the rougher weather. Sadly, one of our patients died just before we reached Pearl Harbour and was buried with full Naval honours. He was very ill when he was carried aboard and it wasn't thought he would survive but it is always a sorrow to lose a man who had just recently gained his freedom.

During the last stages of the voyage, heavy rainstorms were encountered with some rain getting into the hanger to the discomfort of all concerned.

We arrived at Esquimalt on Vancouver Island on 28th October to a fantastic welcome and the sound of two brass bands. Along the Quayside were lines of ambulances waiting to take the sick and they were disembarked first and the fit later in the afternoon.

Canadian newspapers quoted our arrival thus:-

> *"With the aft section of the hanger deck converted into a vast sick bay, Britain's carrier "Glory" ended one of the greatest mercy voyages in history at 10.30 today in Esquimalt Harbor. Carrying 1350 British troops released from Jap camps, 161 Canadian veterans of Hong Kong and 26 civilians, including three Canadians, the Glory tied up at the Naden graving dock".*

Very early next morning, we sailed up the beautiful water way to Vancouver and the Australian VADs delighting in the snow that was falling. For the first time since coming aboard we were able to line the decks with the ship's company and with the Marine Band playing we sailed into Vancouver, where once again we were given a terrific welcome. We had ten days of wonderful hospitality before setting sail on 9th November for our return to Australia but not directly.

We sailed into a dreadful storm after leaving Canada which lasted about three days. Our mighty ship was hurled out of the sea and into the air to come crashing back with a mighty thud into the sea. Everything was battened down but still things were hurled all over the place.

We sailed to Hong Kong where we picked up some Chinese, including women and children who were American citizens to take to Manila. It was not long before they were all very sick and ill and we were involved in looking after them.

At Manila some Dutch troops embarked with their stores to be taken to Balikpapan in the Dutch East Indies. We then sailed down to Tarakan and took on board some Australians.

We were able, on our return voyage, to become involved in the ship's activities and to line the deck when entering harbour with the Marine Band playing which we proudly did as we sailed through Sydney Heads and into Sydney Harbour.

We had been away for two and a half months and covered 24,000 miles voyage on a very worthwhile and rewarding mission and I felt privileged to have been part of it.

HMS Glory *© Crown Copyright/ Ministry of Defence*

Joan David

Joan David was one of our VADs stationed in India for a period of her RN service. This is her story of her time there.

Joyce Drury

HMS Vallura was the largest air station east of Suez. When I was stationed there, having been drafted from RNAH Columbo, the station was preparing for the large scale attack on Singapore which luckily did not materialise as the war came thankfully to an end.

Joan David, Tambaram.

We worked strange hours so as to enable the pilots to have the best of the daylight that was available. We had our breakfast at 5 am and our other meals followed with normal gaps between. It was very good for social life, as one was coming back from a party in Madras it was time for breakfast and to go on duty. So after a bath and change we were ready. When did we sleep? Well, we came off duty at 4 pm, we had a few hours sleep which always seemed enough. It is amazing how during the war we mostly managed with much less sleep and never seemed any worse for it.

When the end of the war in the Far East was announced, we heard the news with great excitement then it was denied. This happened several times until finally the Captain of the Air Station made the official announcement. We were just going to celebrate when our Ward Boy was bitten by a snake which caused a 'slight' panic! He was treated and recovered then everyone went back to celebrating!

Demob started very soon after the end of the war and personnel were being sent back to the UK and the Air Station closed rapidly. In December, being the last VAD nurse on the station, the Wrens having all left, I was sent as an escort to a sick Wren to RNAH Bombay by train. It took two nights and one and a half days. It was a long journey, we were locked in and when the train stopped at a station we were brought food to the carriage. We arrived safely.

I worked at RNAH Bombay until that closed in 1946 when, for a few months, we were billeted in a house at Apollo Bunda, next-door to the Taj Mahal Hotel. We worked in the main hospital in Bombay, where we had a complete floor.

The Royal Indian Navy mutiny took place at this period. Their ships were in the harbour with their guns trained on the 'Taj' Hotel, the gateway to India and our billet. When we went to work, which we did every 24 hours, we had a marine escort in case of an attack. We did have a few brick bats thrown at us but no one was hurt.

A number of the VADs went home, the remainder were drafted to RNAH St Peters, Colombo. We travelled in a hospital train, as it was no longer needed for that purpose. Months later some of us went to Combine Services Hospital, Trincomalee. We returned to England in 1947. RNAS Tambaram is now used for Civil Aircraft. I enquired about it when I went to Madras in 1992.

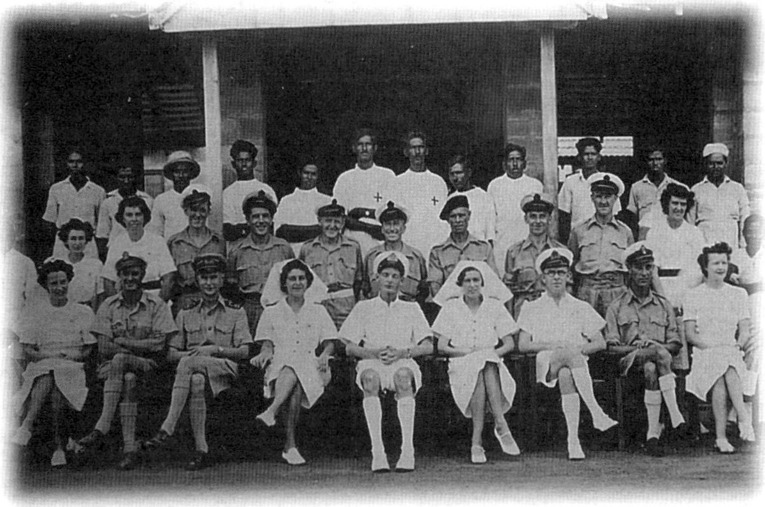

Sick Bay & Sick Quarter Staff, Tambaram.

Jean Smith nee Walker

Jean Smith nee Walker was one of six VADs who left RNH Sydney for Hong Kong to help with the repatriation of Japanese prisoners of war.

Joyce Drury

On 19th August 1945, six Nursing Sisters and six VADs left RNH Sydney for Hong Kong to help with the repatriation of POWs.

On 11th September, we arrived after quite an eventful journey.

The aircraft made a pancake landing at North Queensland (due to a burst tyre on take-off from Brisbane) and as the plane touched down we all ran for our lives expecting it to go up in flames, which luckily it didn't.

Jean Smith 'off somewhere'.

Then an unscheduled landing on a Pacific island where we were not sure until we landed whether we would be met by Japs or Americans, luckily it was the latter.

Our first taste of fruit in Australia 1944.

Stopovers at Manus and Layte and then on board HMS Vengeance and a Hospital ship where we parted company with half our group. Eventually we docked in Hong Kong harbour and were sent to Stanley Camp where the European internees had spent three and a half years in the most appalling conditions. What brave people they were, as of course were the POWs who suffered even worse conditions and were all painfully thin and suffering all sorts of illness.

After a few weeks, when most of the internees had been repatriated, we were posted to the sick bay on M/V Aorangi, a submarine depot ship. This must have been one of the best postings that any RNVAD could have wished for. We were all sorry when in November we had to return to Herne Bay, but it was quite exciting leaving Hong Kong harbour in a Flying Boat.

'TAKING THE AIR' on the flight deck of HMS Vengeance, on their way to take up nursing duties in Hong Kong, are *left* **Sister A M Hippsley, of Wells Somerset, and Nurse J Walker, of Banstead, Surrey, with them is Sub-Lieutenant (A) P Hodgson, of Oxshott, Surrey.** *Pacific Post 22nd September 1945*

Christmas 1944.

Outside our hut: Pegs, Judy, Diana, Joan, Monica, Me and Whiskey & Marjorie.

Ready at last, first few patients have arrived, 1945.

Naina Cox nee Beaven (Senior VAD RN)

In 1944, as a young girl of 16, she was called in by her Red Cross detachment Commandant to be on duty for the influx of wounded on D-Day.

When Naina was old enough she became a Mobile RNVAD and during her service in the Royal Navy became involved in the biggest incident of 1949. HMS Amethyst, a Naval Sloop, was trapped up the Yangtze river, meanwhile the Communists were bearing down towards Hong Kong.

Joyce Drury

Memories Of D-Day Call-Up

Naina Cox nee Beaven in D-day uniform.

I wonder if I was the youngest person officially on duty on D-Day? I was 16 years old and worked in the accounts department of a big firm of dry cleaners in Portsmouth. Due to staff shortages, I was often asked to serve in the shop and saw an amazingly different number of freshly-cleaned uniforms packed up and handed back to their interesting owners; at least 20 different services from all over the world. In 1944, the number of different American uniforms in and out had become noticeable.

At least once a week, from the end of the previous year, I attended Red Cross Classes in the local Baptist Church Hall. This was the Hants 28 Red Cross Detachment, of which I was a member. Our Commandant was Miss D J Hobbs, who had been a VAD in India during the First World War and she did everything to make our attendance interesting. This included asking any Army or Naval Doctor with half-an-hour to spare, to come and talk to us - and help us through our First Aid and Home Nursing exams. I am glad to report that I took and passed every exam going. Small things in the eyes of the world, but a big thing to me.

About 2 pm on June 6th 1944, the shop door burst open. My Commandant found me in the office at the back. "Please, please get permission to leave early and be at the Queen Alexandra Hospital by 5 pm sharp. I have given the

Matron your name and promised you will be there", she said. The Queen Alexandra was the local hospital in Portsmouth, although normally used for ex-servicemen. Reporting on time, I was briskly directed to one of the newly-built Nissen huts. By 6 pm, I had forgotten the number of soldiers whom I had helped wash and feed with warm liquids, both on and off stretchers. By 6.30, I was helping to dress the first bullet wound I had ever seen. These were the first exhaustion cases back from the Normandy beaches. Now I knew what the slow-moving, never-ending convoys of Army lorries were holding. As each one arrived at a hospital hut door, neatly-regimented service boys lifted a helpless body onto a stretcher and these were laid end-to-end, reaching through to any ward with an open door. It was a beautifully fine evening and this helped a lot. By the time it was dark, enough beds had been found.

Later, the Matron sent for me and an older VAD. "Do you have any objection to working on the German prisoners' ward?", she asked. A long silence ensued. Then the other girl said she had a brother fighting abroad and would like to think that if he needed help, someone would give it to him, no matter what the circumstances. This made up my mind for me and I said I would help. We were escorted to the furthest hut, where two armed soldiers standing at the closed outer door stopped us. After checking our names, we went along the tiny passage to the inner doors of the ward, also closed with an armed guard outside. They called the Army Sister, who said one of us would work down one side of the ward with her, the other down the opposite side with the Army ward orderly. By this time we were quicker at changing soiled sheets and washing perspiration off dirty faces and bodies. The main difference in this ward was the atmosphere, so still, scarcely a word spoken, long, long staring looks from pathetically young, grey faces.

My small contribution to D-Day was unpaid, but what a wealth of inspiration it gave me for the future!

Today, most people have no recollection of ever hearing about the 'Yangtze incident', but it played a very real part in my life.

Whilst serving at RNH Haslar, I had volunteered for overseas service and had been told by my Commandant that there were 17 names in front of mine on the list so my chances were almost nil. Also as I was just 21, senior personnel were being favoured.

I went on draft to HMS Heron, Yeovilton, Somerset. The sick bay staff were a friendly crew, with whom I worked well. Compared with other quarters I had been in, the accommodation was very poor, I hated it. The Surgeon Commander and his wife became friends during my short stay and I used to baby-sit for them. The Chief Petty Officer had served in the RNH Hong Kong until the outbreak of war.

At that time the newspapers were full of news about HMS Amethyst. The Chinese Communists had fired on and disabled the RN vessel, killing the

Commanding Officer. Daily conversation was of telegraphist French, who had kept at his post in ever increasing danger sending his signals. He had been serving at HMS Heron and everyone knew him so they were all very concerned.

One day, when I was really fed up, wishing I had not come on this posting, the CPOSBA told me I was wanted on the telephone. It was the Medical Director General. "Would you sail for Hong Kong in three weeks time?", the business-like voice said. A very unsteady me stuttered with excitement, "If you can assure me that this is not a mistake, yes, I will go, also how is it that only a short time ago I was told there were many in front of me and my chances were nil?" The reply was straight to the point, the volunteers in front of me were put off by the situation out there either by their own minds or their relatives. A willing volunteer would be more use than a pressed VAD. My thoughts were, 'nothing could be worse than working in my present posting'.

News travels like bush telegraph in places like this and by lunch time, everyone knew I had volunteered. The Surgeon Commander came to see me and told me I must be out of my mind going out to what was obviously a very nasty situation and also I hadn't a clue what I was letting myself in for, he did, because he was in Hong Kong when the Japs left and had first hand knowledge of how the Chinese fight. He begged me to change my mind, he offered to ring the MDG for me and take the blame! I sent a telegraph to my parents asking for permission to go, (these days girls would not do this, but our parents were still an important part of our lives and we would not like to disobey them). My mother used her persuasion on my father as she had wanted to join the WRNS in the first war and her parents forbade it. I heard later that my father had been horrified at the thought of me going.

It took only two days for everything to be confirmed, then joy of joys my warrant arrived. Now I was ready for the off. The sick bay staff, whose company I had enjoyed, shook hands with me and wished me the best of luck, the Surgeon Commander chipping in with, "... and how you will need it!". We still had to travel in uniform although the war was over. En route for Portsmouth, I was joined by two officers in what had been an empty carriage, one RM, the other RN. Both duly commented that I would be better off staying at HMS Heron! Can you imagine that being said today when girls are in combat on the front lines of action? Ah, but this was fifty years ago and things were different then.

After a long weekend at home, a little strained, I knew my parents were worried, but I had an underlying excitement within me which I couldn't explain. Then off to report to RNH Haslar. I was given temporary accommodation in one of the old wards which had been converted for the war time VADs and were nicknamed by them as 'horse boxes' because there was just enough room for an iron bed, locker and chair, with a partition each side. I had forgotten all about inoculations which had to be endured in quick succession for going abroad. I cannot name them all. Typhus was awful, yellow fever made me so ill that I was thankful just to lie back in my 'horse box' bed for a couple of days. Next I was told to get my tropical uniform together and was even given a small allowance towards buying it. Fortunately, I found out in the nick of time that we could wear WRNS officer white drill dresses for daytime overseas hospitals as they were similar. These could be obtained from naval stores which were vastly cheaper compared with civilian shops, as were their white buckskin shoes, so beautifully made and not expensive. For my white velour hat, I had to visit Scotts in Old Bond Street, London. This was a wonderfully unforgettable experience and I felt I was growing up at last. On entering the shop I was greeted by a well-mannered vendeuse who knew exactly what I required, sitting me down at a dressing table, using hand mirrors so skilfully, making sure the size was correct and that I was happy with the result. She added the corded silk band and the bright metal badge. After that, my first visit to Harrods to buy two uniform dresses.

Then home on leave. At home the new steel trunk was delivered, then mother and I packed this to the brim and father solemnly painted my title and name on it in white. Large official labels had arrived and these had to be tied and stuck to the trunk 'HMS Troopship Dilwara' clearly visible. Without fuss, a naval lorry collected it.

A few days later, picking up my hand luggage, my mother and I wended our way to the Gosport ferry, crossed the harbour, took a bus to the Main Gate at Haslar and said our goodbyes, actually without a word being said.

So on the first of June 1949, naval transport took me to Southampton dock. Whatever the troopship was to others, I neither knew nor cared, to me it was a floating white palace. Less than four years since the war had ended and I

Naina is pictured here on troopship Dilwara holding the chalk.

had known only grey war torn ships and blacked out lights. Five Naval VADs were part of the compliment of that troopship which was filled to capacity. The Oxfordshire & Buckinghamshire regiments were, at the time, the best trained to cope with any problems which might arise around Hong Kong. The communists were gradually pushing South from the Yangtze river area. The RNH Hong Kong was due for staff changes because some of the VADs had completed their two-year contract. Usually there was an almighty clamour from young ladies serving in RNHs in the UK to fill these vacancies since this was a 'plum' draft. I walked up the gangway, showed papers and pay book, a Goanese steward showed me to a cabin. Scarcely had I time to take in the details, when three other VADs arrived, all older than I, (in fact I was to be the youngest at RNH Hong Kong for six months). We were unknown to each other and each had been hoping for an individual cabin. This was a full ship, sailing for a very serious reason. However, we were in the first class cabins and probably had more room than most. We four agreed that the food in the dining saloon was first class in every way and afternoon tea was served in pre-war style which was a delight I will always remember.

After a few days smooth sailing, the ship was engulfed in a Bay of Biscay storm. It never affected me one jot, I must have had some seafaring blood in my veins. I went to get ready for dinner. The others were in their bunks, so I had the little bathroom to myself without the need to hurry. It never occurred to me that anything was amiss and that they were seasick. On entering the saloon, I found I was the only one to be having a meal!! One waiter escorted me to my table, one pulled out my chair, another unfolded and placed my table napkin, different waiters brought my drink and each successive dish. Nothing like it ever happened again. I really enjoyed the attention. I felt like a royal princess. Eventually the Senior Purser joined me to explain that sea-sickness had claimed everyone else. Then we sat in the lounge swapping stories about ourselves. At one stage, a very young Army Officer appeared briefly to snatch a brandy and ginger ale and then scuttled away!

First port of call was Salonika, Greece. Most of us could remember our fathers talking about this place. They were here in the First World War. We wanted to go ashore but nothing had been organised. A St John VAD and myself sat on the top deck and enjoyed the sun. Two Army Officers had been able to organise a small covered lorry in order to deliver documents and packages to a barracks. We didn't need asking twice when being invited to go with them. After their business was over, with a little time to spare, we took a chance and drove way up into the hills. He had been there before. A small taverna served some kind of sparkling drink and we had great fun paying for it counting out thousands of drachma, the rate then was thirty two thousand drachma to the pound sterling.

Back on board, we learned we were bound for Port Said. It was everything the story books had said - there weren't many travel books about in those days. Simon Artz and Turkish Delight were enchanting.

On to Ceylon, seeing the palm fringed coast of Columbo in the early morning mist was a sight to behold. There were many traders lining the way to old charabancs for a small fee off to Kandy to see the Temple of the Tooth ceremony. On our return we saw the tea picking and elephants bathing.

The arrival at Singapore was quite exceptional with the strains of 'A Slow Boat to China' played by the Scottish Regimental Band as we sailed in. No lack of organisation here - representatives of all the services were waiting to show us around. Visits to 'Happy World', 'Golden World' and many others, dancing on a black glass floor, very fascinating, at the Mountbatten Club, then on for drinks at 'Raffles'.

Four days later, Kowloon, Hong Kong. First our mail from the Purser's office. Then the usual disembarkation routine. 'Coolies' took our suitcases, the RN dealt with our trunks from the hold, all to be ready at the RNH for our arrival. The journey from the ship to the hospital could have made a story of its own. We boarded a tender which took us leisurely across the harbour to HMS Tamar, a small Naval bus drove slowly through Wanchai, up through a higher road, followed by a slow ride to the peak. Our destination the Royal Naval Hospital. No-one had really prepared me for the magnificent view from here, words would not be sufficient to describe it, so I will leave it to your imagination.

Everyone was on duty when we arrived, the Red Cross Commandant, Mrs Barbara Hall, formally received us. After a quick freshener, we sat down to a late lunch, then were shown to our cabins. Once again we slept in part of a ward, this time very light and spacious with proper doors.

Through the last month, none of us had forgotten the reason we were on this journey, although we had not received much news of events up to now. We had time before they sailed on their journey home to say farewell to the parties we were relieving. Our Commandant gave us all a cocktail party so it was a hello and farewell function. It was a big affair with all the official RN present. My thoughts were, 'Even if I'm bombed by the Communists next week at least I've lived a little!'

My travelling companions were appointed to different wards and I to the Senior Wardmaster's Office, Percy Silk the SWM was attached to the Surgical Capt. J G Maguire's offices which were one side, then Miss Muriel Cawston, our Matron on the other. My position here was to deal with all the 'bed tickets', in fact they were the medical files. Endless queries and problems arose which I had to deal with. I was often go-between for doctor and patient. Also dealing with personal documentation and drafting. It took me several days to get used to the work. Then, what we had been working and waiting for - HMS Amethyst had broken free! - estimated time of arrival in Hong Kong uncertain. We were on standby. Two days later, a great air of excited tension, the ship would arrive about 11 am. With a bit of contrivance I was able to join the welcoming group at the dockside at HMS Tamar. HMS Amethyst was coming into view. It was something I could not have missed after this long journey and anticipation. She limped into harbour like a huge injured creature of the sea, magnificent in her agony, a great hole had been blasted in her wounded side. This had been skilfully mended from the inside with mattresses by the shipwrights and ratings to make her seaworthy. Shoreside sailors willingly helped dock the ship, her own crew were worn out physically and mentally, the strain they had been under was absolutely impossible to imagine. They had spent all those weeks trapped up the Yangtze not knowing what was going to happen next. It was only professionalism which had saved the day and of course a lot of courage. The Governor of Hong Kong, Sir Alexander Grantham and Sir Robert Ho Tung were the first to greet Commander Kerans. Ambulances were waiting with sick bay staff in attendance. Many of the ship's company needed hospital treatment not just for wounds but general conditions. Within an hour I was back at my desk at RNH. I could not believe I had been present at this historic moment. To have seen the Amethyst limp into harbour after that heroic escape from the Yangtze under cover of darkness, such a part of history to relate to my grandchildren (there have been books written and films made on the Yangtze incident for anyone who is interested).

Now it was down to work with much fervour. All doors to the Surgeon Captain's office, Matron's and mine were locked and a guard posted at the entrance. There were so many secret documents to be dealt with. Our connecting rooms had their own facilities which was fortunate as we worked for fourteen solid hours on medical reports and the crew's personal reports on the confrontation up the Yangtze. We were brought refreshments every so often which were very welcome. To be honest, it didn't seem like fourteen hours. All this information was relayed to the Admiralty in London, signals were flashing back and forth and the lines were red hot. I may have been sworn to secrecy but what I typed was utterly riveting with interest. After this marathon of duty, most of the next day I slept, all the nursing staff were too tired to talk, it had been a very hard stint of duty for everyone.

Within a week, tension in the atmosphere lightened and we were invited to a dance at the China Fleet Club by the ship's company, the official incidents were never referred to.

I still have copies of the Daily Graphic with photographs taken on the day the troopship left England, also a copy of the China Mail with photographs of the Amethyst.

I got to know the telegraphist from 'Heron' quite well and was able to tell him how his ex-colleagues had worried and talked about him before I had left England. He was given Admiralty promotion for staying at his 'key' for many dangerous hours.

There were many awards given to HMS Amethyst's crew, not forgetting the ship's cat who, although slightly wounded, carried on killing the rats which were attacking the food store. The Dickin medal was awarded for its courage.

I spent two years in Hong Kong. It was an experience I would not have missed. Some of the restrictions on us seemed petty, such as having to be in so early. They would not have been tolerated by the young women of today. We were all used to discipline in the RN and took it as part of our life.

VAD's Royal Naval Hospital, Hong Kong, visit of Lady Louis Mountbatten, Naina is in the centre, immediately behind Lady Mountbatten in her best uniform. 17th March 1950.

Alfreda Etheridge

Alfreda Etheridge is one of our long serving VADs. This is her story of service on HM Hospital Ship 'Maine' during the Korean War.

Joyce Drury

Memories of HM Hospital Ship 'Maine' 1953

It all began in 1949 when I was drafted from RN Hospital Haslar to RN Hospital Chatham to replace a Head VAD who was to join the hospital ship 'Maine'. Little did I think that four years later I should join the ship.

Early in July 1953, four VADs boarded the Troop ship that was taking soldiers out to Korea. After about a month at sea the troops were disembarked in Pusan, South Korea. The ship then went on to Kobe, Japan where the 'Maine' was docked. We four VADs were replacing the four VADs on the 'Maine' who were due home after completing their two years afloat. After a few days in Kobe the 'Maine' sailed for Sasebo on the coast of the outer island. About the middle of August, hostilities had ceased in Korea and casualties grew less. From then onwards our patients were the usual routine cases from the ships. We VADs nursed the Officers. At first it seemed difficult nursing them in cots - but we soon got use to it!!

Life was generally pleasant 'on and off' duty. Our living quarters were two large cabins, one day and one night. The night one was like a small dormitory with five bunks, a small bathroom and galley. Two Chinese Mess boys looked after us. We worked split duties and off duties were ample. When we went ashore we went by Liberty Boat, as the 'Maine' was anchored at sea and the trip took about 25 minutes to reach Sasebo quayside. We shopped in the American PX Store there and had our hair done. Film shows for the staff were shown on deck in the evenings. Outings were arranged for the Ship's Officers and Nursing staff when duties allowed. On a visit to a Pearl Farm I was the only lady in the party and an oyster was opened and I was given the pearl. My pearl was made into a ring which I still have.

Boat drill was a regular event, and in early December the 'Maine' set sail for Hong Kong. During the second day at sea, the whole ship's company were summoned to their Boat Stations and the ship searched. A little Japanese girl stowaway was found in the hold. What happened to her once we reached Hong Kong, I never knew.

After our arrival in Hong Kong, our patients were transferred to RN Hospital and we were allowed a rest period. On Christmas Eve Matron, Sisters and VADs joined the carol singers from HMS Tamar, the shore base and went carol singing with them. First to the hospital then to the ships in the harbour, before attending Midnight Service in "Tamar" Church. On Christmas Day, we joined the Ship's Officers, Medical Officers, Matron and Nursing Sisters for a Celebration Lunch in the Wardroom. Sadly a few days later we left the 'Maine' for duties in RN Hospital, on the Peak. The 'poor old ship' was eventually broken up as 'She' was found to be unseaworthy. How sad after all that service.

Alfreda stayed in the Royal Navy until 1965, although the VADs were disbanded in 1960, she stayed to help train new intakes and do administration work.

Haslar 1949

Kindly lent by Velma Charleston, Christchurch, Dorset

Some of the other interpretations of the initials VAD (Voluntary Aid Detachment) by the sailors:-

Virgin Awaiting Destruction

Virgins Almost Desperate

Very Able Darlings

Virtuous And Demure

Acknowledgements

I would like to say thank you to the following people:-

Gordon , for all the support he has given.

Andrea, for all the interest she has shown and her support.

Rod, for being my legs.

Gordon's office, for all the willing help I have been given from all the staff.

Dudley Reference Library, for giving me willing answers to my questions.

District Library Service, North East Fife District Council.

Dorothy Foxley nee Ingleson, for hearing my appeal for VADs over the radio.

Charlie Chester, for broadcasting it on BBC Radio 2.

Sheila Eastell, for her help.

My postman, Glenn Downton, for all the extra mail he has had to deliver over the months.

All those who have lent photographs.

And many thanks to all the ladies and gentlemen who have written for me to make this book so interesting.

Author's Postscript

Our lives together were hard but enjoyable. We learnt a companionship which still remains. There was always a colleague to go out with or someone who would listen to our problems. This has been the story told by the young women themselves and blended together to become the life as a VAD.

I have found myself dropped into a 'time-slip' putting this book together, reliving a part of my youth which held such a mixture of happiness, sadness and exhilaration.

I am almost sorry the story is finished and ready for the printers. It will leave an empty space after such a busy period.

Now you have finished the book and read of our work and journeys, I trust you too have been dropped back to a war time not of killing but healing.

There have been a lot of 'hiccups' on the way, illness and burglaries included. Anyone who has tried to have a book published will know the ups and downs and hold-ups that can occur, frustration is the word when it is out of your control. With a lot of help and hundreds of telephone calls we got there to have 'We Were There' published.

Joyce Drury